CURRENT OPPORTUNITIES
AND FUTURE VISIONS

Reflections
on Lasallian Higher Education

Reflections
on Lasallian Higher Education

EDITED BY

Craig J. Franz, FSC

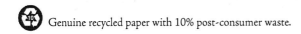 Genuine recycled paper with 10% post-consumer waste.

Publishing team included Craig J. Franz, FSC, editor, David Ford, Secretariat, and manufacturing coordinated by the prepublication and production services departments of Saint Mary's Press.

Printed in the United States of America.

ISBN 978-0-9787250-0-6

To order copies of this publication, please visit ialu.smp.org or phone 800-533-8095 in the USA; outside of the USA phone +(1) (507) (457-7900).

CURRENT OPPORTUNITIES AND FUTURE VISIONS: REFLECTIONS ON LASALLIAN HIGHER EDUCATION

Table of Contents

PREFACE

The global impact of Lasallian universities is enormous. Each day approximately half a million people are educated within this remarkable system. Lasallian universities provide quality instruction and values formation in the time-honored educational tradition inspired by Saint John Baptist de La Salle.

Organized collaboratively as the International Association of Lasallian Universities (IALU), these higher educational institutions operate an impressive number of diverse educational entities and offer a wide variety of undergraduate and postgraduate areas of study. They are united in their desire to extend and enhance De La Salle's vision. Together, they promote excellence in Catholic higher education while providing innovative opportunities for collaboration, research, exchange, and development.

During the IALU regional directors' meeting of July 2005, a decision was made to share perspectives from around the world regarding the future of Lasallian higher education. The timing seemed propitious. There was increased interest by lay partners in administering universities, yet they needed to know what challenges lay ahead. The Brothers of the Christian Schools would be conducting a General Chapter (2007), during which time information would be needed regarding the role of Lasallian universities around the world. Additionally, as the membership of IALU discusses future actions at their triannual Encuentro (2007), they would need to be aware of global issues influencing Lasallian higher education on different continents. It was from this confluence of needs that

Current Opportunities and Future Visions: Reflections on Lasallian Higher Education was born.

The regional directors invited a select group of seasoned authors to think broadly and deeply about the future challenges and opportunities that would be shared uniquely by Lasallian universities. To respectfully preserve the diversity of responses, the text, divisions, and footnotes remain in the formats of their original submission. IALU is appreciative of these authors sharing their thoughts with fellow colleagues via this publication.

The enclosed compendium of perspectives divides somewhat naturally into two categories of responses. One group provides comments relative to global concerns in higher education (Cervantes, Franz, Hengemüle, DeThomasis, Ojeda). A second group discusses developing issues in Lasallian higher education relative to particular institutions (Johnston, Quebengco, Choquet, Gómez Restrepo, Aguayo.) The introductory essay by Landeros sets the stage for the essays in this volume by providing valuable background information on IALU and Lasallian universities globally. In a similar fashion, Rummery's article provides concluding possibilities for continuing Lasallian research, investigation, and development.

Joan Landeros begins our analysis by comprehensively examining the historical development of Lasallian university education from its beginnings. The notoriety which Lasallian higher education exhibits was gained only in the 1990s. Landeros explains how networking has become so important at this time and provides insight into how essential those networks have been and will be for Lasallian universities. She offers hope and encouragement for how such networks might strengthen the work of IALU and higher educational institutions around the world.

José Cervantes insightfully posits the question, "Will the Catholic university survive, and, consequently, will the Lasallian university survive these postmodern times?" He proposes ten characteristics specific to the Catholic university and then contrasts them with the challenges of postmodern times. His thoughtful analysis reflects major trends that influence the presence of the Catholic university as "an indispensable alternative for living a healthy pluralism in the world of education."

Craig Franz talks about five themes that provide both opportunities and challenges for Lasallian universities. His reflection begins with a brief overview of the development of higher education in the Lasallian world. He then discusses the need to fully engage associates, mature our social consciousness, remain faithful to innovation, retain our institutional uniqueness, and leverage the kinetics of globalization.

Edgard Hengemüle explores the constitutive elements that characterize a Lasallian university (especially in light of De La Salle's pedagogical influence largely being directed toward the primary level). He carefully examines the elements of faith, community and service as espoused by the Founder and later incorporated into our universities. Finally, he concludes by solidifying a series of widely held expectations about Lasallian higher education that influence its development today . . . and in the future.

Louis DeThomasis uses Gabriel Moran's tension between the two understandings of the word *end* (meaning or substance v. finality or termination) as a backdrop for his development of the characteristics of Lasallian higher education. He argues for systemic solutions to social injustice and emphasizes the need for Lasallian education in times of heightened religious fundamentalist ideologues. He concludes with reflections on how Lasallian universities should foster new ideas, understandings, and paths to knowledge within the Church.

Juan Antonio Ojeda discusses what will be necessary for Lasallian universities to transform themselves into vibrant educational communities in an evolving world. Through organic changes in the cultures of our institutions, Ojeda suggests that we will be able to distinguish ourselves as outstanding educational institutions. His eight themes suggest some very pragmatic ways in which we might wish to proceed as Lasallian universities collaborate more efficiently.

John Johnston examines Christian Brothers University in Memphis, Tennessee, USA, as an example of a Catholic, Lasallian university. In his essay, he analyzes thoroughly the way in which the university lives out its Catholicity concomitant with a diverse student body composition. His pertinent thoughts are helpful for any Lasallian higher educational institution, and his concluding implications chart the nexus between Catholicism and Lasallian university administration.

Carmelita Quebengco's essay begins by providing background information on De La Salle's development of schools and then focuses on work in Asian higher education, with particular reference to the Philippines. There are significant challenges when a university seeks to be simultaneously adaptive and formative. Quebengco's discussion of shared mission and Lasallian association form the second half of her essay as she explores current realities and posits developing possibilities for the future.

Philippe Choquet talks passionately about the potential for international cooperation among Lasallian universities. He cites his own institute, the Superior Agricultural Institute of Beauvais, and its decision to change its name to La Salle Beauvais Polytechnic Institute, to better highlight its Lasallian mission. Choquet takes a global view in his discussions on growth, and he suggests a series of factors Lasallian universities must consider if they are to continue providing additional educational opportunities around the world.

Carlos Gómez Restrepo uses an understanding of Latin-American education as background for the rationale as to why the Lasallian Educational Project (PERLA) was developed. The project is based on five principle points: the explicit proclamation of the Gospel, the democratization of knowledge, sustainable human development, defense of the Rights of the Child, and the promotion of justice, peace, and the right to life. His essay highlights the distinctiveness of the PERLA project with regard to other educational initiatives.

Enrique Aguayo looks at Universidad La Salle in Mexico City and examines the philosophical and pragmatic aspects constituting that Catholic, Lasallian university. Of particular interest is his examination of the framework of peaceful coexistence on the campus and the elements that characterize its solidarity. As a recurrent theme, he discusses how students of significant financial means can and should be educated alongside poor students in Lasallian schools.

Gerard Rummery concludes our perspectives by reviewing the unique characteristics that extend De La Salle's vision into higher education. He encourages us to know, appreciate, and revisit the founding story in our continuing educational work. Rummery cites a number of areas of current Lasallian research and talks of possible areas of future investigation for Lasallian institutes of higher education.

This book is being published in both English and Spanish to ensure access by a wider audience. Translations of the essays were completed in México at Universidad La Salle and we are especially grateful to the following translators for their hard work: Iván Nelson Angues Bambarén, Br. Blasio Donato Hillenbrand, Helene Albrechtsen, Hilda Cortes, Nanette DePaoli, Pilar Rangel, y Joanna Sepúlveda.

IALU is appreciative of the willingness of the publisher to produce and distribute *Current Opportunities and Future Visions: Reflections on Lasallian Higher Education*. When I approached John Vitek, president of Saint Mary's Press, about this project, he immediately provided his full personal and professional support, for which I am most grateful. We appreciate the many others at Saint Mary's Press who similarly greeted this publication with dedication and enthusiasm. Saint Mary's Press has a strong reputation for producing Catholic publications of the highest quality, and IALU appreciates their collaboration in this current project.

Finally, the authors of this book hope their ideas stimulate productive conversation among all who are associated with Lasallian higher education. While the authors can suggest possible scenarios for the future of Lasallian higher education, the dedicated individuals who partner together every day at our universities are the ones who thoughtfully sculpt the shape of their Lasallian university. We hope that, in some small measure, the thoughts conveyed in these essays are helpful in that process.

Craig J. Franz, FSC
Editor

TOWARD THE CREATION OF A LASALLIAN INTERNATIONAL UNIVERSITY NETWORK: PROGRESS AND PROMISE

By: Joan Landeros

There is a photograph on the wall in the main corridor of the Mother-house in Rome of a statue of Janus, the Roman god of portals and patron of beginnings and endings. More than just a curious glimpse of Roman history, it is a reminder of the importance of recognizing the past and considering the present while looking to the future. Representations of Janus portray him as having eyes, nose, and mouth on both the front and back of his head, symbolizing that a doorway or portal can be simultaneously an entrance and an exit. As Janus stands in a doorway, the present, he can look forward and backward at the same time.

Lasallian education has passed the threshold into a new millennium and a new age of interconnection. It can be proud of the centuries of accomplishments. Hopefully, this threshold will mark the beginning of an energized international commitment of Lasallian higher education to create a network that will sustain the worldwide Lasallian educational community.

Br. Álvaro Rodríguez, Superior General, opened his address to the Encuentro VII of the International Association of Lasallian Universities assembled in Barcelona on January 14, 2004, with these words: "My presence among you is intended to be a sign of the importance our Institute gives today to higher education and an act of faith in its enormous possibilities. In the history of the Institute, the growth of Lasallian universities in almost all the regions of the world is without precedent, and is a sign of the times, which we cannot ignore."

1

Recognizing the Past

The place of Lasallian higher education is coming to the fore in the Institute. Only recently have there been explicit reflections regarding the historic place of higher education in the evolution of the Institute. From the vantage point of three hundred years hence, it has become obvious that advanced, specialized education has always been a fundamental element for the Lasallian educational mission. Br. Álvaro Rodríguez also reminded the presidents and rectors of IALU that "in a certain way, we can say that higher education in the Institute was born with the Founder and his concern for the formation of teachers." Education of his own Brothers as teachers and education of rural schoolmasters were early initiatives that showed his response to the concrete educational necessities of his times. The constant training and perfecting of the Brothers' professional skills and spirituality was the Founder's focus and has been part of the Lasallian charism long before our modern-day reference to lifelong learning.

De La Salle's proposition of salvation through education was not static. He offered inspired pragmatism: seeing the reality of the circumstances, trusting in God's providence and guidance, and committing to transformation, which historically has led the Institute to inspired innovation. Even before the French Revolution, the Brothers had developed specialized options and pedagogical strategies beyond the primary level. Early in the nineteenth century, they had begun working in secondary education and evening adult classes for workers. Agricultural education was also started in this period. The Agricultural Institute of Beauvais opened in 1854. During the following decades, trade and commercial institutes were founded, not only in France, but also in Europe and North America. In the second half of the nineteenth century, tertiary Lasallian education was well established through institutions or, their predecessors, like St. Luc, Brussels; Manhattan College, New York; La Salle University, Philadelphia; and St. Mary's College of California; among others.

Universities have always claimed to be international institutions; nevertheless, most of those institutions founded since the mid-nineteenth century have been, in fact, national and, in many cases, primarily regional institutions. With local and regional focus, it is understandable that colleges and universities did not begin to consider themselves as globally connected institutionally until the onset of information technology and pervasive globalization made the world a village. Lasallian universities have not been an exception.

Although the international migration of Lasallian education has included all levels of instruction and many kinds of ministries through education, national and regional conditions directly influenced the development of Lasallian higher education and the character of its relationship with the Institute for over a century. With the most notable exception of the Philippines and Bethlehem, where the Brothers came from abroad to specifically take charge of university education, Lasallian institutions of higher education were founded at the invitation of local bishops or by the extraordinary initiative of a few Brothers, and were considered exceptional to the mainstream activities of the Brothers, primarily involved in basic and secondary education as well as formation. Until quite recently, there has been a persistent questioning of the legitimacy of higher education in the Lasallian educational mission.

It is important to note that the Institute's first call to action, directed specifically to Lasallian institutions of higher education, was by the 42nd General Chapter in 1993. The signs of the times were marking a new era for higher education. During the late 1980s, the boom of new Lasallian universities began in Latin America and the Philippines. Demographics and demand for specialized and tertiary education were also pressuring long-established Lasallian institutions to create branch campuses and to reach out to new constituencies. In addition, in many areas of the world, especially in developing countries, teacher education was gradually being officially incorporated into higher education, which began to close the real, or perceived, distance between Lasallian higher education and traditional Lasallian educational ministries. All facets of the Lasallian educational mission were responding to paradigm shifts caused by globalization and internationalization. Being attentive to the needs of the times, it was not surprising that in 1993 the capitulants looked to a force within the Institute, which had begun to consolidate a unified presence: the Lasallian institutions of higher education. Solutions to the causes of poverty and social injustice needed researchers. Preservation of the environment required specialists. Collaboration with international organisms needed intermediaries (Brothers of the Christian Schools, Circular 435, pp. 25–26, Rome, Italy). The time had come when the universities had to accept these Lasallian challenges, not only on a local level but also as a unified, international force.

The pressure to internationalize and to engage collaboratively with diverse sectors, agencies, and institutions did not come just from the center of the Institute. The phenomena of the rise of universities joining together to form multilateral consortia became more prevalent in the 1980s and increased exponentially through the 1990s, parallel to the development of regional trading blocks, such as NAFTA, MERCOSUR, and the integration of the European Community, and their increasing needs for strategic intra- and interregional collaboration. Higher education, as the classic motor for development, was enticed by programs such as Erasmus, ALFA, the North American Mobility Program, etc. The growth of these consortia over the past twenty years also reflects the growing recognition of the impact of globalization on higher education and the need for the internationalization of institutions to better integrate outside perspectives, implement delivery methods accessible to a broader range of students, share scarce resources, and systematically engage with international corporations, governments, nongovernmental organizations, and other higher education institutions.

The combined group of Lasallian institutions of higher education was not oblivious to these forces. During this same period, collaborative efforts within the Institute's regions began with greater intensity and purpose. It became obvious that there was a unique competitive edge in joining forces in a united Lasallian effort, rather than competing with one another.

LACUP, the Lasallian Association of College and University Presidents, has brought together the North American Lasallian higher education representatives for a growing agenda of mutual concerns and cooperative efforts. In Mexico, ILMES, *Instituciones Lasallistas Mexicanas de Educacion Superior,* has united the interests of now fourteen institutions of higher education. Through RELAL, *Región Lasallista de América Latina,* universities in Latin America have communicated and collaborated on projects of mutual institutional interest as well as regional development, most notably the PERLA project. Similarly, the Lasallian superior technical institutes and universities from Spain, France, and Belgium have met regularly, not only for projects promoted by the European Union and the Bologna process but also because of the added benefits of their shared heritage, tradition, and strategic unity. In the Philippines, the De La Salle system has grown to over 70,000 university students. Lasallians have formed part of the Australian Catholic University. The collaboration of Lasallian higher education in the Asia Pacific Region, PARC, has been expanding, and a new tertiary institution has been founded in Indonesia.

The presidents and rectors of Lasallian institutions of higher education had met as an international group since the late 1970s, but it was during Encuentro V (1995) and Encuentro VI (1998), both held in Rome at the Generalate, that the necessity of creating a representative, international organization came to maturity. The International Association of Higher Education, IALHE, was founded under the leadership of Br. Craig Franz, then president of Saint Mary's College of California. Awareness of the true international dimensions and character of Lasallian higher education became dramatically apparent at the individual institutions within the regions and throughout the Institute. By the turn of the millennium, most of the Lasallian colleges and universities were comfortably referring to themselves as international and as members of the international group of Lasallian institutions of higher education. In many of the districts, the educational mission began to seek complementarity, rather than autonomy, between ministries and levels of education.

By the 43rd General Chapter, in 2000, the recommendations to the universities and tertiary-level institutions were clear, precise, and vital to the future of the Institute. Research was requested on the conditions of education around the world and of the characteristics of Lasallian higher education. Support for the Rights of the Child, a renewal of the Lasallian values, the proclamation of the Gospel, and the promotion of ecumenical and interreligious dialogue were just some of the recommendations made to the whole Institute, but it was clear that the talents and capacities of Lasallian higher education had opened great expectations (Brothers of the Christian Schools, Circular 447, Rome, Italy). University representatives have served on the permanent Standing Commissions for the Lasallian Educational Mission and on Association, and have participated in the preparation of the first International Lasallian Assembly, scheduled in 2006, anticipating the 44th General Chapter in 2007.

The existence of an identifiable international organization of Lasallian higher education was empowering. As the lines of communication were strengthened and greater knowledge was disseminated, the level of activity began to increase exponentially among the members. Encuentro VI, 2001, in the Philippines, was distinct because it was a gathering of an association, not just a meeting of representatives of individual institutions. Regional directors were elected, goals were set, and vision had been given by the recent Chapter. The reelection of Brother Craig gave needed continuity of leadership.

The unwieldy IALHE/AIILES designation was changed to IALU/AIUL, International Association of Lasallian Universities/Asociación Internacional de Universidades Lasallistas/Association Internationale des Universités Lasalliennes—international, inclusive, and united.

Considering the Present

Until the last decade, the reference to the worldwide Lasallian group was true in essence and in potential, but not too much in consequence. This is not to say that individual institutions or the regional groups were not engaging internationally. Nevertheless, the interaction among Lasallian universities had been minimal outside of the regions until the Association began to bring together members of specific interest groups at the La Salle Conference Center in Cuernavaca, Mexico. Soon thereafter, specialized groups began to organize meetings to move ahead on their own collaborative agenda. This has been the beginning of the unique Lasallian higher education international community, a network of networks.

By 2004, Encuentro VII, in Barcelona, the representatives of Lasallian higher education, had a common logo, a *mapa mundi*, with all the members of the Association graphically present. Academic vice presidents, vice rectors, and provosts had come together, as well as staff and faculty responsible for Lasallian formation, deans and directors of the business schools, and directors of campus ministry. Each institution came with tangible experience of the existence of a greater Lasallian international whole. Even if the institution did not directly participate in the activities sponsored by IALU, they received from the Association, the District, and the Institute, bulletins, newsletters, announcements, and visited the Web page, which created a new consciousness of an evolving interconnected community.

It has been providential that the opportunities for Lasallian institutions to come together through IALU have coincided with a number of common social, economic and institutional realities facing higher education worldwide. Those realities include the call for internationalization of colleges and universities, the recognition of the positive and negative impacts of globalization on education, the advent of the Internet—which has transformed the paradigms for communication—the need to combine resources and create partnerships for institutional sustainability, development, and effectiveness, the increased demand for study abroad and academic exchange, and the preeminent necessity to collaborate and learn with colleagues around the world through teaching and research. As Lee Sternberger recently wrote, "It would appear that the final factor, our collective interdependence, is the principle paradigm driving all of the collaborative arrangements. There is little doubt to administrators, faculty, students, policy-makers, and funding systems that the future truly belongs to those who seek to understand different world views and establish international partnerships with institutions of higher education across the globe" ("Partnering for Success," *International Educator*, 2005, vol.14, no. 4, pp. 12–21, Washington, DC).

Even though Lasallian institutions are competing strategically internationally to meet the contemporary challenges of quality and pertinent higher education, fidelity to its founding heritage gives coherence to its higher education community through an identifiable set of characteristics and values commonly shared throughout the world. While the diversity of the Lasallian higher education community mirrors the complexities of any multilateral, multicultural network, there is a distinct advantage of sharing a common educational mission. Nevertheless, difficulties of language and intercultural relations still exist. Economic asymmetries prevail, as well as a wide variety of stages of institutional and systematic development. Since each institution was created to meet specific needs at a particular moment in history during the last 150 years, it would be ludicrous to assume that every Lasallian college and university would be able to respond similarly in every circumstance.

In an analysis of the initiatives that have been undertaken among Lasallian institutions of higher education, a foundation of trust, communication, and commitment have marked the most successful partnership, even among very distinct institutions. Trust may appear to be a popular buzz word for business analysis, strategic planning, sales, or even international education, but without it, networking and collaboration would be impossible. Trust is not instantaneous, even in an organization that shares a common vision. It takes time to know one another and each other's institutions. Communities and networks cannot develop or make progress without trust. Communication is essential to develop a project with the adequate balance between vision and strategy. Specific and ongoing attention has to be given to organizational and systematic processes and to the practical realities of the program or project, its design, implementation, and evaluation. Fortunately, institutions with more experience and expertise in program and project management have take leadership roles in creating viable collaborative networks between various regions in the IALU world. Communication and information technology has facilitated the rapid development of consortia, programs, and projects and has helped to maintain frequent and routine dialogue. Commitment is the magic third element identified by analysts of successful collaborative initiatives. Commitment must come from the top down. Collective trust and commitment must be encouraged and shared among all the participants. They, in turn, must share their experiences with their constituencies in order to create confidence in the viability of future Lasallian networks.

The panorama of Lasallian institutions of higher education collaboration can be distinguished by a wide variety of activities, of which the following are a few examples:

- Student mobility has expanded not only in number but also in the diversity of participating institutions and kinds of academic exchanges. LACUP now offers a study-abroad consortium that pools their international program offerings. Bilateral agreements have proliferated among the Lasallian group to facilitate more student participation in exchanges through tuition waiver. Short-term special-study programs are increasing each year, as are shared social service programs, internships, and experiential learning programs. Credit transfer and recognition of academic equivalencies has become easier as staff have become more familiar with partner institutions.

- Promotion of graduate programs within the Lasallian international group has become prevalent due to the improved communication network, new recruiting efforts, and a greater familiarity with international opportunities. As an example, La Salle Barcelona offered scholarships to graduates from sister institutions. Ninety-six students were recruited in one year from Mexico alone for their master's programs.

- An international MBA program shared between the United States, Mexico, Europe, and the Philippines has resulted from the Business School Deans' conference in Cuernavaca. Undergraduate business majors can now study two semesters abroad at Lasallian institutions and receive a diploma from the IALU.

- The Lasallian International Research Network (LIRN) was organized in 1999 by De La Salle University Bogotá, as a result of the first Cuernavaca meeting of academic vice presidents the previous year. The network now comprises eighteen Lasallian universities from Latin America and Spain. This science and technology network has participated in ALFA projects and has continued to organize thematic meetings as well as videoconferences. Recently, the LIRN/RIILSA network had been opened to the entire Lasallian group of colleges and universities.

- Lasallian engineering schools have taken the initiative to meet to combine efforts and integrate infrastructure and services. Christian Brothers University, Memphis, TN, has convoked a meeting to move forward on the "Lasallian Global University System," which intends to extend Lasallian higher education to the entire Lasallian community around the world. This is a significant step because Lasallian collaboration is moving from bilateral and regional online projects to an international, holistic vision of all levels of the Lasallian educational mission, utilizing communication and information technology without sacrificing the fundamental values of Lasallian pedagogy.

- The Centro Superior de Estudios Universitarios, Madrid, is proactively promoting the creation of knowledge networks throughout the IALU. After an extensive itinerary of visits to Lasallian universities, the following lists of networks have been proposed by the participating institutions: presidents/rectors, technology platforms, doctorate in education, educational institution management, international cooperation-project management, facilities management, education, special education, intercultural relations, significant learning, social work and community development, Lasallian formation, international relations, access, occupational therapy, research, nursing, international commerce, advanced training for lawyers and judges, innovation parks, small businesses development, environment, agriculture, food technology, and university programming for seniors.

- Lasallian volunteer efforts have begun to integrate. The Lasallian volunteer movement in the U.S. has begun to collaborate with Mexico to complement areas of talents and needs. International Lasallian volunteers can be seen all over the globe. Just as there has been an increase in academic mobility, networks for social service and attention to the poor and needy have become internationalized on Lasallian campuses.

- The International Lasallian University Leadership Program will begin in June 2007, at the Casa La Salle, Rome. The theme "Lasallian Partners in Catholic Universities: Enhancing Understanding, Eliciting Commitment" shows the new energy on the part of Lasallian higher education to fully embrace the shared mission of the Institute and promote Lasallian association. LACUP is helping to sponsor the initiative, but the invitation is to all IALU member institutions:

> To be of continuing service to the Institute through the exploration of interrelationships among faith, service, and culture, as well as to better respond to the needs of our students, we feel the need to establish a university-level formation program. This program of formal studies would enable participants to consider contemporary Lasallian themes while building community among an international cadre of talented and committed faculty and staff. This experience will seek to deepen one's personal faith while providing opportunities to work with marginal populations or other fundamental Lasallian needs of the day. Ultimately, participant groups— together and by association—will serve as animators in their respective universities and districts, serving as leaders for the integral human and Christian development of the students entrusted to them." (Br. Craig Franz, FSC, president of IALU, *Prospectus on University-Level Formation*, June 22, 2005, Cuernavaca, Mexico)

Looking to the Future

Sociologist Manuel Castells, in his book *The Rise of the Network Society*, focuses on the revolutionary information and communication technologies that emerged during the last three decades of the twentieth century. He observes that as the Industrial Revolution gave rise to the "industrial society," the new Information Technology Revolution is now giving rise to an "informational society." He argues that the recent information technology revolution has given rise to a new economy, structured around flows of information in global networks. Castells also observes that throughout society, networking has emerged as a new form of organization of human activity. He has coined the term "network society" to describe and analyze this new social structure.

The author states that before attempting to reshape globalization, we need to understand the deep systemic roots of the world now emerging. He goes on to propose the hypothesis that all major trends of change constituting this new, disconcerting world are related, and that sense can be made of their interrelationship. In spite of a long tradition of sometimes tragic intellectual errors, he insists that observing, analyzing, and theorizing is a way of helping to build a different, better world (Felix Stalder, *Manuel Castells*, Cambridge, UK: Polity Press, 2006).

The Lasallian international group of institutions of higher education is, indeed, becoming part of the network society. The emerging Lasallian global connections are using the inspired pragmatism of the Founder to see the needs of the times, analyze—yet trusting in divine guidance—and commit to transformation in order to move the shared Lasallian educational mission ahead.

The new reality of interconnection within Lasallian higher education, supported by new information and communication technologies, is also creating pervasive social networks within and beyond individual institutions. Each communication creates thoughts and meaning, which give rise to further communications. Fritjof Capra, in *The Hidden Connections*, observes that this is the way networks become alive and self-generating. This is how the Lasallian networks of higher education are helping to generate living networks within the entire Institute. Lasallian higher education is contributing to, and benefiting from, the production of common contexts of meaning, shared knowledge, values, and conduct, which are now defining the Lasallian family of the future. Communication, trust, and commitment are assuring the success of this expanding interconnectivity.

Organizational theorist Etienne Wenger has coined the term "communities of practice" for self-generating social networks. He refers, though, to the common context of meaning rather than the pattern of organization through which the meaning is generated. Wenger explains that as people pursue any shared enterprise over time, they develop a common practice of shared ways of doing things and relating to one another that allows them to achieve their joint purpose. Over time, the resulting practice becomes a recognizable bond among those involved. Capra adds that within every organization, there is a cluster of interconnected communities of practice. The more people are engaged in these informal networks, the more developed and sophisticated the networks are—consequently, the better the organization will be able to learn, respond creatively to unexpected new circumstances, change, and evolve. The organization's vitality resides in its communities of practice.

This is precisely the strength of the Lasallian network of networks. Lasallians share thousands of diverse communities of practice all over the world and yet are recognized distinctly as Lasallian. Responding to the needs of the times will always mark the new life generated by Lasallians everywhere, who work "together and by association." As we look through the portal of Janus, we can see the future of Lasallian higher education as the creator of the networks and a vital connection throughout the entire international Lasallian family.

Author Biography

Dr. Joan Landeros is director and founder of the Center for International Education at La Salle University in Mexico City. A former Fulbright scholar and a British Council scholar, she has been teaching at Universidad La Salle in Mexico City since 1973. Dr. Landeros is a member of the Standing Committee for the Lasallian Educational Mission in Rome and serves on the Executive Committee of the International Association of Lasallian Universities.

Bibliography

Capra, Fritjof. *The Hidden Connections.* New York: Doubleday, 2002.

Brothers of the Christian Schools. Circular 435. Rome, Italy, 1993.

————. Circular 447. Rome, Italy, 2000.

Rodríguez Echeverría, Álvaro, FSC. "Reflexiones 65: La Educación universitaria dentro de la Misión Lasaliana," *Reflexiones Universitarias, Ediciones Universidad LaSalle.* México, DF, 2004.

Stalder, Felix. *Manuel Castells.* Cambridge, UK: Polity Press, 2006.

Sternberger, Lee. "Partnering for Success," *International Educator,* vol. 14, no. 4. NAFSA: Association of International Educators, Washington, DC, July–August, 2005.

Wenger, Etienne. *Communities of Practice.* Cambridge University Press, 1998.

THE FUTURE OF THE CATHOLIC UNIVERSITY FACING POSTMODERN TIMES

By: Br. José Cervantes, FSC

The university is the only human institution that has lived uninterrupted for almost one thousand years. It has not only survived change, the university itself has provoked many of the changes. Its survival has not been accidental. On the one hand, the university has been able to form the new cadre of leaders of society, and on the other hand, it has been able to maintain its ideals while being fairly critical of society and of itself.

But there is no guarantee that the university as a Catholic university will continue to survive. The university was born Christian in a Christian social context. It survived the Renaissance, Enlightenment, and Modernism under different forms. When the university became secular, the Catholic university as an alternative to the secular university experienced difficulties in attaining its goals.

The institutional presence of the Catholic Church today in the world of higher education is impressive—almost one thousand institutions. Its presence is most clearly evidenced in the United States, India, and Latin America. Of note is the case of the Philippines, the only Catholic country in Asia where the Catholic university has a significant presence.

The Catholic university has survived only by affirming its mission, namely, proposing Christ as the model and prototype of the human being as based on the inspiration on the Gospels.

Many are of the opinion that the Modern Age has entered into its decline. Its proposals of well-being and knowledge for all have been a failure. Neither technology nor science has resolved man's basic problems.

Will the Catholic university survive, and, consequently, will the Lasallian university survive these postmodern times?

This is the key question of the following reflections and one that I have asked myself, as a consecrated person experienced in higher education, for at least thirty years. As a Brother of the Christian Schools, I also ask myself the same question, convinced as I am to champion this privileged mission. In this paper I propose ten characteristics specific to the Catholic university, and I will contrast them with the challenges of postmodern times.

1. Faced with postmodern times, where it makes no sense to think about meaning, the Catholic university offers a complete vision of existence.

Globalization has given knowledge previously unrecognized importance. All education that concentrates only on production, efficiency, and competition debases the human being. Of course, the economy regulates educational demand, but we run the risk of not taking care of the true nature of the human being, ignoring his essential needs. "Man does not live by bread alone." The model of the human being is debased in many educational offerings.

The Catholic university educates the most profound dimension of the human being, the spiritual-religious, which is the only dimension that can guide the university student in his/her search for the ultimate meaning of life. This is a great responsibility, since the credibility of the ultimate proposal of the Catholic university is based on the credibility of all the other aspects of the university, from sports and academics to the buildings themselves.

There can be no "total vision of existence" if the Catholic university, in this case specifically Lasallian, does not have a serious department of philosophy and a department of religion. There can be no "total vision of existence" if there are no philosophy or religion courses in the standard curriculum and that those courses are not optional subjects or merely the finishing touch, but rather an integral part that serves as the base to challenge the other courses that make up the core studies.

For the postmodernists, the death of Nietzsche's god that held the death of man, the modern subject, is behind us. Today, neither the *ergo cogito* of Descartes nor the *transcendental* subject of Kant nor even the *absolutism* of Hegel are viable. Postmodernists affirm that all of that is erased by the *system* (Luhmann) and the *structure* (Foucault), thus breaking with the traditional concept of man.

According to the postmodernists, since progress no longer exists, it makes no sense to think about meaning. There no longer is a project because there no longer is any subject to project; history no longer exists. The subject is alone: he exists only in the present.[1]

Before these questionings and challenges of postmodernism, the Catholic university needs to find serious, credible answers and alternatives.

2. In the supermarket of "value bargains," the Catholic university generates and develops values stemming from the Gospels.

It is fashionable today to talk about values. We have seen the rise of proposals that not only lack an ultimate meaning, but don't even come from a cosmovision *(weltanschauung)*, or even a philosophy, much less from a specific axiology.

Currently, in spite of postmodernism, one can still see, often simultaneously, diverse tendencies in values-education:

- The neo-Kantian or neo-Fichtean *idealistic* tendency that reduces the human being to a pure mental category. The ultimate end is pure subjectivism.

- The *realistic* or *phenomenological* tendency that considers that values exist as a "being in itself," not as an intellectual intuition, but as an emotional intuition. This is the position of Max Scheler.

- The *psychologistic* tendency that sustains that values are relative, since they are based on inclinations and affectations of the subject.

---

[1] Vattimo, *El fin de la modernidad*. G. Lipovetsy. *L´ère du vide*, Paris, Gallimard, 1983.

- The *sociologic* tendency considers that values are mere "social facts" and are analyzed as any other social fact that can vary from society to society. Therefore, values are completely relative.

- The *existentialistic* and *liberal* tendency maintains that values are created by freedom without any norm or objective reference. Freedom of the individual is the supreme value.

- The *metaphysical* and *spiritualistic* tendency sustains that values have a fundamental reference to spiritual activity and to the relationship with the Absolute, who is manifest in human reality. In the search for human values is born a search for the metaphysical essence of the value. Value is a revelation of the Absolute.

This basic typology is useful for clarification, but in real life, it almost never appears in pure form. The tendencies operate as combined, successive alternatives. Sometimes behavior is based on one tendency, other times on another.

The Catholic university, in this case the Lasallian university, manifests its uniqueness by affirming with deeds the characteristic defined as "value" in education. To educate today is to go against the current. The *laisser faire* tendency in education is the grandchild of the permissive grandparents of the sixties. If indeed every university can promote certain values, the Catholic university generates, transmits, and teaches values that are derived from the person of Christ himself in the Gospels. Further on, reference is made to this *testimonial* aspect.

3. Faced with utilitarian offerings, the Catholic Church operates with a purpose toward salvation.

The Church has always considered the university as a means to search for truth and, therefore, the complete truth—the TRUTH, with capital letters. The Catholic university fulfills the purpose toward salvation. It is a place that makes possible the clear message, the knowledge of Christ and his Church. It facilitates the dialogue between faith and culture. In the varied typology of existing private universities, universities were created by companies to fill their needs; others are "businesses" and a family or institutional patrimony (a case in point, the University of Phoenix that defined itself as a "not-for-profit institution"). There are also those that promote an ideology or a religion.

The Catholic university, without ignoring any of the administrative and organizational disciplines, does not seek profit, invests as much as possible in the institution, and is concerned about tuition costs as well as economic aid to those in need.

Christianity emphasizes the profound dignity of the human being and the values that it undertakes in cooperation with others. It points out that existence has meaning that transcends, even though it is based on reality and in its own personal history.

> The modern progress of science and technology, which due to its method cannot penetrate into the ultimate causes of things, can foment certain phenomenism and agnosticism when the method of investigation employed in these disciplines is wrongly used as the supreme rule for finding all truth. Moreover, the danger exists that if man is overly trusting of present-day inventions, he will begin to believe that he is self-sufficient and stop his search for higher causes. (*Gaudium et Spes*)

A controversy exists as to whether a Catholic university can really call itself a "university." Let us remember, as was stated above, that the university, due to the social context of the moment, was born Christian. Today the situation is totally different, but the offering of the Catholic university has known how to evolve in order to maintain its significance in a secular, plural, and even hostile world. It has overcome the apologetic stage in order to be the bridge between faith and science, between faith and culture.

The quality of the Lasallian university and its profound respect for other philosophies, ideologies, and religions has gained it respect and consideration, not only in the Western world but also in the Muslim world.

As Finkielkraut affirms in one of the few studies of the postmodern phenomena and its implications for education, the university requires an adjustment at all levels. This applies not only in the area of values, attitudes, and habits, but also in content, since only that which has an operative and utilitarian character will be accepted. "The rulers of tomorrow will have to invent, and, above all, they will have to allow the act of inventing."[2] Everyone knows that today's economy, as well as tomorrow's, is based on information (it is received, dealt with, transmitted . . .). While it uses little energy and few raw materials, the information economy demands a large number of well-trained people.

4. Faced with intolerance and manipulation, the Catholic university creates an environment of freedom and respect.

The Catholic-Lasallian university is not known for excessive religious practices nor proselytizing. Today the universities of Christian inspiration reflect an atmosphere of humanism based on freedom and respect. The Lasallian university is Catholic in origin and inspiration. Its purpose is clear and defined, and it is extremely respectful of other options. The identity of the Catholic university is clear and precise, since only from clear identities is dialogue between different cultures and disciplines possible.

For many years Catholic universities, present in Islamic or non-Catholic countries, have been models of a defined presence and a respectful attitude toward surrounding different religious and cultural environments. This has gained them admiration and respect.

The problem that is presently facing the Catholic-Lasallian university, and it will be more so in the future, is how to be itself with its Catholic identity and, at the same time, be open to all currents of thought; how to sympathize with the concerns and pain of human beings and, at the same time, maintain its own characteristics.

---

[2] Finkielkraut, *La derrota del pensamiento*, Barcelona, Anagrama, 1987.

In today's world, outspoken groups and ideologies exist that criticize and contradict the Catholic university's source as Christian inspiration. These groups not only demand attention, but also are very aggressive in their proselytizing.

At risk is not merely a respectful or civilized coexistence, but rather the discovery of how to live in solidarity under these circumstances.

According to the postmodernists, the bourgeois man has died, but that also applies to the proletarian man. The "I" with its phobias and attachments no longer exists, but neither does the "we." Existential or social problems, such as the struggle of the classes, no longer exist. Technology that marked the anthropological and social processes of the twentieth century has succumbed to a social vacuum. The turbine has given way to the computer. Means of production are now means of reproduction. Today, it is said that alienation and anxiety have disappeared, but aloneness, social fragmentation, and isolation have multiplied. Students base their personal vibes on sports, speed, risk, aggression, and the vortex of bars and clubs on the weekends.

And the university? The Christian stance? It has not escaped the accelerated rhythm of the postmodern ideology. Possibly the worst symptom of this is the absence of the fundamental axiology in many of its proposals, both on a formal and an informal level.

Education in the postmodern era has entered into a struggle for its constitution and legitimacy. It has been threatened in its own identity. On one side is the university and on another very different course are the social relations of the students and more than a few faculty members.

Thus contradictions are lived: relativism is opposed by rigidity and the unity of the plans of study, the speed of changes is countered by the perpetuity of classical science. The absurdity and disinterest produced by the humanities is opposed by the desire to find a spiritual substratum.[3]

And what is the alternative? Postmodernize the university? But isn't postmodern the same fiasco of the university and formal education?

---

[3] Jamesson cited in Vattimo in *La sociedad transparente* (page 76)

Nobody has the answer, but everyone asks the question. In the Catholic university, these ideas must find a way to be discussed and circulate, under penalty of denying reality and missing the boat of life once more.

5. Faced with religious ignorance and generalized superficiality, the Catholic university offers systematic religious knowledge at the university level.

Religious sociologists have catalogued traditional religiousness as devotional and of little incidence in the moral life of people. Even on the professional level, there is an abundance of crass ignorance when it comes to the matter of religion. Many of the difficulties that a Catholic faces are not derived from faith but from simple ignorance.

Among the traits of postmodernism is the culture of image and simulation. Respect for mystery and profound reflection have been lost. A unified vision of history has disappeared. All vital experiences seek an emotional substratum or they have no meaning. Skepticism, demythification, and desacrification predominate.[4]

Our universities, through the appropriate courses on the university level, specifically promote the religious formation of our students. The courses of Christian formation as well as the departments of campus ministry should take into account the postmodern university when planning activities. It is of little avail if the university, with its rationality, its sense of history, and its faith in science, continues to be modern, but the university students are postmodern.

6. Faced with the denial of what is transcendent, the Catholic university facilitates dialogue between faith and culture.

The university, as a seeker of truth, cultivates knowledge, learns about different cultures and disciplines, and establishes a respectful dialogue with

---

[4] Lyotard, *La condición postmoderna*, Madrid, Cátedra, 1987.

them. Facing the profound crisis of evidence and credibility (according to Fukuyama, we are at the end of utopias), the Catholic university brings the illuminating presence of faith not as a theoretical reference, but as the vital expression of the search for meaning. It is as *Ex Corde Ecclesiae* states: "the institutional presence of the Church in the world of culture."

By nature this dialogue is difficult. The spheres of science, culture, and faith are autonomous, but they don't have to be irreconcilable. Each one from their specific content, methodology, and objective can and must dialogue without feeling threatened. On the contrary, cloistered faith is the extreme opposite to a Catholic university student's attitude.

I have given classes in law, psychology, sociology and ethics to Catholic students. I know how difficult it is to make these postmodern youths understand that there are absolute values, that ethics are not subjective, and that faith is the real connection between man and what is transcendent. That Christian faith cannot be lived without love. That it is the only way we can discover the meaning of life and death. That the encounter between God and man is a new way to "be on earth." That law and legal precepts do not justify us. That Christianity is not a series of legal precepts. That there is no opposition between the sacred and the profane. That if they repeat, "Do what you want . . . ," Saint Augustine already said something similar but totally different: "Love and do what you want . . ."

And where else, if not in a Catholic university, in a Lasallian university, are students going to discover and favor these new Christian attitudes that are hard to understand by many postmodern youth and future professionals?

7. Faced with growing differentiation, the Catholic university is the crucible of the new society.

When the Catholic university doesn't enclose itself predominantly in one social class, but thanks to specific programs is generally accessible, it becomes a crucible of a new society, where all social classes meet, dialogue, and coexist. In this way it establishes a new type of human coexistence and contributes to fill the gaps of separation between social classes, political parties, or religions. It revolves around a new society in which respect and love are ascendant.

I think it would betray the very essence of the universality of the institution if it became classist or elitist. Even though the university may have many social development programs, these would become merely public assistance.

8. Faced with the lack of commitment and solidarity, the Catholic university supports its proposal with a testimonial reference.

A while ago, in a nationwide survey designed to update the mission of a well-known university institution, I was asked about the strengths and weaknesses of the institution. While there were many strengths, only one "weakness" emerged that they recognized as clear-cut: that of not having a testimonial group of persons witnessing the values they propose.

The Catholic university has this strength; its first reference is Christ, the model person. But, in addition, congruency among the teachers is also called for, so that purpose and life be coherent in both their personal and social lives. This is no easy task. *Ex Corde Ecclesiae* proposes at least three levels of congruency:

1) to ask faculty and personnel to respect the proposal
2) to ask that they adhere to it
3) to invite them to commit themselves to it

Many Catholic universities have achieved the formal and group commitment of many of its components, both with faculty and students, namely to live and promote Christian institutional inspiration. It goes without saying that this active, committed presence exerts a beneficial influence on all the university community.

Today, many of those who study human conduct have reevaluated the role model of adults. Agreed upon or not, the teacher is an accessible reference for students. This becomes a benefit when the teacher is a witness to Catholic values.

9. Faced with commercialization and profit of knowledge, the Catholic university, precisely because it is a nonprofit enterprise, evokes the contributions and commitment of many sectors.

The message of almost all Catholic universities is very clear: it is born of the unified effort of many people. From the initial dream of one person or a group of people, Catholics, sometimes religious congregations, the hierarchy, and socially responsible businessmen, join together. They all come to the conviction that only by being united will they be able to carry on. They discover that in solidarity is strength, that a new type of education is possible if solidarity is the base.

In fact, many Catholic institutions experience a new sense of belonging in connection with a group of people from which an alternative project of education arises and for which, they, in unity, will be responsible.

Postmodernists speak a great deal about society as a "system." This is not anything new in sociology. The difference is that for Luhmann, systems are not composed of people but of communication. Basic to his theory is the concept of "autopoiesis," the internal dynamic, the auto-activity of the system. Neither philanthropy nor solidarity is typical of many cultures. There has been some advancement, however, in this area in almost all cultures. Undoubtedly, one of the sources of the Catholic university's vitality resides in the fact that it was born of the solidarity of so many groups and people.

10. Faced with the multiplying number of alternatives and the confusion of ideology, the Catholic university is a model of predictability.

If living the Christian life aids the unrelinquished prophetic role, the Catholic university carries it out on the corporate and institutional levels. In an economic, political, ideological, and ethical dilemma, social dealings have become very complicated. In many we have lost the consensus on issues such as gender, sexual identity, and the roles of culture, economy, political platforms, multiculturalism, and minorities. By definition a

Catholic university is a place where identities are built and moral values are formed. It cannot escape openly stating its position on these aspects. Because of its prophetic role, the university must discuss and question all proposals.

To be critical, the Catholic university has a horizon, which is hope, and a reference, which is the Gospel. The criticism covers everything: mind, heart, thought, and action. Hope demands of the Catholic university that it be present in the transforming actions of society. Every human project must be submitted to criticism.

Often our critical proposals can be threatened by the subtle play of power and be in conflict with the "establishment." It is an unavoidable risk that does not entail the abandonment of one's duties. Neither can we ignore the high risk that may exist when teachers and students defy existing beliefs, ideas, and values. Such was the position of Christ in his Sermon on the Mount.

The critical attitude of the university opens a door of freedom to discuss the conventional boundaries and questions that arise in society. The Catholic university, based on its name, is neither neutral nor apolitical. Nor, at the risk of sacrificing its nature, is it partisan. The Catholic university in the function of its prophetic role can take many forms, but it favors compassion and social responsibility, having as its goal the conquest of the possibilities of greater human happiness and a more critical citizenry, so that justice reigns in all relations, and economic and political democracy becomes a reality.

Conclusion

According to Fukuyama, in the postmodern era there is no place for utopias, and we are facing the end of history.[5] Personally, I believe that the day we have no more utopias, humanity will disappear. I think that the

---

[5] F. Fukuyama, *La fine Della storia e l'ultimo uomo.* Rizzoli, Milán, 1996

Catholic university, in its systematic form of searching for the presence of the Gospel in culture, is the most beautiful of all utopias. In a free and democratic country, the presence of the Catholic university is an indispensable alternative for living a healthy pluralism in the world of education. But, "the worst that can happen to salt," says the Master, "is that it lose its flavor." The presence and action of the Catholic university in our society is an undeniable urgency because

- It has the Gospel as a reference.

- It considers the human being as the subject of salvation.

- It seeks the freedom of the individual.

- It finds in culture a privileged form of evangelization.

- It considers society as its sphere of operations.

Today, postmodernism challenges the proposals of universities, in particular Catholic universities, just as the Renaissance, Enlightenment and Modernism did in their times. Will they respond to this challenge? If the Catholic university is not able to meet that challenge, it may disappear, but if it is able to respond to these new issues of humanity, a long life awaits our Catholic-Lasallian universities.

Author Biography

Br. José Cervantes has served as president of the Mexican Federation of Private Institutions of Higher Education, as Visitor of North Mexico, and as General Counselor to the Superior General in Rome. A distinguished leader in higher education, he was a founder of Universidad de Monterrey, ULSA Noroeste in Obregón, and ULSA Chihuahua. Three times serving as university president, Brother José headed Universidad La Salle institutions in Mexico City, Obregón, and Chihuahua.

Bibliography

Chomsky, N. y Dieterich H. *La sociedad global.* Joaquín Mortiz, México, 1995.

Colom Antoni J. y Mèlich Joan-carles. *Después de la modernidad.* Paidós, México, 1997.

Finkielkraut. *La derrota del pensamiento.* Barcelona: Cairós, 1988.

Foster H. y Habermans, J. *La posmodernidad.* Barcelona: Cairos, 1985.

Habermans. *El discurso filosófico de la modernidad.* Madrid: Taurus, 1991.

Jamesson, F. *El posmodernismo o la lógica cultural del capitalismo avanzado.* Barcelona: Paidós, 1991.

———. *Posmodernidad y sociedad de consumo.* Barcelona: Cairos, 1985.

Lipovetsky, G. *La era del vacío. Ensayos sobre el individualismo corporativo.* Barcelona: Anagrama, 1990.

Lyotard J. F., *La condición posmoderna.* Madrid: Cátedra, 1987.

Touraine, Alain. *Critique de la Modernité.* Paris: Fayard, 1992.

Vattimo. *La sociedad transparente.* Barcelona: Paidós, 1990.

———. *El fin de la modernidad.* Barcelona: Gedisa, 1986.

TRUE TO A VISION, STEADFAST TO A DREAM

By: Br. Craig J. Franz, FSC

The Brothers of the Christian Schools have been involved in teaching youth for more than three centuries. Initially responding to a call of providing primary education to young boys, the noble educational mission of the Brothers has expanded greatly and now encompasses a rich array of schools across six of the seven continents, in more than eighty countries. From kindergarten to higher educational institutions, the Brothers of the Christian Schools—at different times and in different ways—have responded creatively to the call to serve those who otherwise would be denied such educational opportunity.

During the first two hundred years, the Brothers typically established primary and secondary schools for youth. During the past century, however, their educational zeal and visionary spirit has birthed numerous higher educational institutions (see the appendix at the end of this essay: Global Growth in Lasallian Institutions of Higher Education). While to some, this migration into tertiary education represented an unanticipated movement into a new frontier, the involvement of the Brothers of the Christian Schools in higher education was, and continues to be, a wise, appropriate, and necessary extension of the Lasallian mission to provide educational opportunity to those in need.

Living in the era of great thinkers like Jean Jacques Rousseau, Thomas Hobbes, Denis Diderot, and Voltaire (Francois-Marie Arouet), the Founder, Saint John Baptist de La Salle, was an engaged participant in the intellectual trends of the French Enlightenment, which hailed change and progress as good. De La Salle was both an innovative man and one who was fiercely dedicated to the best interests of those entrusted to his care. Those two qualities—innovation and dedication—have continued to hallmark Lasallian education around the world. When De La Salle decided to teach in French instead of Latin, he broke the mold. When he taught grouped classes of students rather than a single individual, he broke the mold. When he developed textbooks to facilitate learning, he broke the mold. When he set up schools to teach the poor gratuitously, he broke the mold. To a superlative degree, Saint John Baptist de La Salle modeled educational innovation. Responding to the signs of the times, he had the courage and vision to create new educational models.

Lasallian Higher Education Today

While the roots of our Institute may have been in those primary and secondary schools, the acute sense of responding to the times through innovative pedagogy has been a dominating force in Lasallian higher education as well. Today, our universities are well known for their strong pedagogy that expertly links theoretical constructs with practical needs. While our institutions are rich intellectual centers in their own right, they are also grounded in the need to merge theory with practice. In doing so, they provide an environment that blends both the visionary intellectual constructs of free thought and the pragmatic practices of commonplace realities. In these Lasallian schools, education has married application.

Our institutions often address themselves with particular sensitivity to needs of the local area. Where knowledge of agriculture is needed, our institutions are engaged in farming and research so as to strengthen the local community. Around the world, Lasallian higher education institutions are educating miners, oceanographers, farmers, doctors, lawyers, engineers, scientists, teachers, ministers, nurses, dentists, executives, judges, and many other professionals . . . innovatively linking the latest in academic knowledge with practical implications for immediate use. Indeed, our institutions have become centers for incorporating both important knowledge and ethical understanding into the fundamental fabric of the societies in which we operate.

Lasallian institutions of higher education are well known for their outstanding quality of engagement. In all of our tertiary institutions, students value highly their exposure to dedicated faculty. They appreciate the human, caring touch such faculty bring to instruction. They learn far more than just the materials relegated to a subject-specific area: they learn ethics and values in every class. Our students appreciate the warm engagement that is generated organically by both dedicated faculty and caring staff. Lasallian tertiary institutions that offer residential facilities are additionally known for the quality of compassion and hospitable care that is given students as they develop healthy intellectual habits of the mind in the academic wing of the university. On each campus, there is a holistic fusion of integrated components so as to provide the best possible experience for students.

The innovative nature of our Founder has not been lost in the three centuries of our existence. Quite the contrary, innovation in tertiary education is one of the features that characterize our contribution to higher education.

Around the world, higher educational institutions respond to the signs of the times through the development of new programs and opportunities for study. Riding the crests of the diverse and challenging educational waves, programs in a variety of areas are being fashioned creatively. Central and South American countries host fresh programs in informatics. North America boasts new programs in geospatial information, even while the essential software is still being developed and improved. Philippine programs in conflict mediation are being developed to assist with negotiations in the conflict-rife areas of the Pacific Rim. Through constant improvement models, the quality of education is always alive with change. Integrating such change in rapidly evolving areas of knowledge demands constant updating, reassessment, and renewal. Some students excitedly report that majoring in these areas of rapid innovation is akin to flying an airplane at the same time the engines are being changed!

Innovative programs are not limited to a single subject area. New ways of teaching and new understandings of the cognitive learning patterns of adults have enabled our institutions to reach out to adult learners effectively and successfully. Our institutions offer graduate programs along with postgraduate educational opportunities. Web-based courses enable those who cannot engage in traditional classes the opportunity to gain training and degrees asynchronously at convenient times and locations. Creative interinstitutional programs in business bring together students from one continent and allow them to receive instruction on other continents at sister Lasallian institutions. Innovation and creative pedagogy are alive and well within tertiary Lasallian education.

Lasallian colleges and universities around the world also realize the need to provide an atmosphere where reflective thought can help guide conversations and the development of one's faith. Lasallian institutions strive to be safe and welcoming places for individuals to examine their personal spirituality. Regardless of whether the students are Roman Catholic or not, our environments must continue to be places that foster the spiritual development of students, encourage the practice of one's faith, solicit the thoughtful examination of religious understandings, welcome interfaith dialogue, and make palpably present the religious nature of the campus. The faith life of the Brothers, staff, and faculty help to model an integrated life in which one's encounter with God through scripture, sacraments, and community service make visible the underpinnings of a vibrant life of faith.

Looking Toward the Future

As one looks toward the next decade of growth in Lasallian tertiary education, common themes will emerge that provide both opportunities and challenges. Although the degree to which any particular institutions may be impacted by these trends may vary from one location to another, all Lasallian institutions of higher education will wrestle with these issues in the years ahead. They are (1) engaging our associates, (2) maturing our social consciousness, (3) continuing faithfulness to innovation, (4) retaining our institutional uniqueness, and (5) leveraging the kinetics of globalization.

1. Engaging Our Associates

Thanks to the extraordinary dedication and life-giving interest on the part of lay associates, the Brothers of the Christian Schools have been able to expand and enhance their tertiary educational offerings. Known in different areas by different names (partners, associates, lay colleagues, etc.), these enthusiastic individuals provide a rich array of talent, energy, and vision for our institutions. Their increasing involvement has brought a fertile and hopeful new meaning to the phrase "together and by association." Through the collaborative interaction of such partners, institutions have blossomed in previously unanticipated ways.

In some areas of the world, this increased involvement has coincided with concomitant growth of qualified Brothers to assume university administrative and staffing responsibilities. In other cases, when the traditionally generous and talented pool of Brothers has been diminishing, devoted partners have grasped the baton and resolutely kept our institutions moving forward. The rich talent pool of lay colleagues often has offered superior choices for key positions. Particularly in the United States, and other regions more generally, the movement of dedicated partners into key university leadership positions has been one of the most hopeful signs for the continuance of De La Salle's work that we have seen in decades.

So as to ensure there are no interstices in the ongoing expression of Lasallian mission in our institutions, lay partners must be familiarized well with the history and mission of the institute. Into their hands many of our institutions will be commended. What has been so very gratifying for Brothers around the world is the fervent interest our lay colleagues have in understanding—and living—the Lasallian mission. These women and men become emotionally, pragmatically, and spiritually connected to the Lasallian mission in a way that is redolent of Shavuot, when, in the Pentecost event, the Apostles had tongues of fire resting on each of them and they were "filled with the Holy Spirit" (Acts 2:4). Indeed, the zeal of lay colleagues today coincides with a pivotal institutional moment as our worldwide religious congregation transforms itself into a worldwide educational movement.

The plurality of personal and communal lifestyles (married, single, celibate, widowed, single gender communities, mixed communities) on the part of our partners within a very well defined mission brings both richness and texture to the fabric of our mission. Where previously the responsibility as guarantors of the mission resided in the Brothers, this task now is increasingly, willingly, and capably assumed by a wide array of individuals. Not only in our educational institutions, but also in the Church as a whole, lay involvement has shown remarkable growth. As Peter Steinfels says, "Not since the fall of the Roman Empire have lay people taken such an active leadership role in the Church." These inspired and devoted masses do not merely speak of their faith . . . they act upon it.

Although diverse perspectives can offer better ways to read the signs of the times and adapt institutions to them, such diversity can also lead to division. To ensure that institutions continue to move forward and do not become mired in controversy, it will be necessary to continually provide associates access to formation, core Lasallian texts, Lasallian spiritual practices, and mission related activities (retreats, prayer groups, pilgrimages, etc.). Indeed, visionary Catholic leadership must reify theology.

Though we tend to think of faculty and staff as the principal source of lay colleagues, it would be unfortunate for us not to include alumni, parents, and friends in our considerations. Students who have graduated from our schools become some of the strongest supporters of Lasallian education. Through engagement with faculty on a daily basis, their history results from the summation of many positive experiences. They had many years to personally witness the impact a Lasallian education can have on one's life and they often show remarkable understanding of and dedication to the Lasallian educational mission. Parents, similarly, see the transition in their child(ren) and have great appreciation for the Lasallian environment that caused such positive and transformational change.

Friends familiar with the ends of a Lasallian education are often inspired to work with us in this remarkable ministry. In the future, these resources will be increasingly more important in supporting Lasallian institutions physically, financially, and spiritually.

It is important to ensure that we hire for mission. Faculty must be brought to our institutions who not only demonstrate competence in their specific area of expertise, but also bond with us emotionally and spiritually in De La Salle. Similarly, staff should be solicited who are engaged on numerous levels with the Lasallian mission of the school. Clearly, people recognize a Lasallian institution not only by the signs at the entrance, but also by how individuals engage each other within the institution. Hospitality, honesty, and a supportive student environment thrive in such locations. In continuing to keep such characteristics abundant, steps must be taken continually to ensure that Lasallian institutions demonstrate appropriate values and actions, both broadly and deeply.

One cannot assume that because the leadership of an institution is firmly rooted in the Lasallian tradition, the institution will also be rooted. It is the collectivity of individual actions throughout the school that determine the nature of the institution. Although executive-level leadership is essential in directing the movement of an institution toward or away from a Lasallian mission, the cumulative influences of myriad faculty and staff may be as important, if not more so, than that of any single authority.

2. Maturing Our Social Consciousness

Pope Pius XII prudently commented that if one wants peace, it is important to work for justice. Inspired by this viewpoint, and owing to the ongoing discussions of Catholic social thought in our institutions, there is an increased desire for academic and religious understandings to serve as underpinnings for enhanced social action. Increasingly, students want to see our faith put into action by outreach to the local (and sometimes regional or national) community. To them, a litmus test of our sincerity is our commitment to social action.

Though the exact mechanism and direction by which this action should be taken is sometimes a matter of administrative concern, this integration of action with one's faith and knowledge is a very positive sign. Upon graduation, our alumni should be "ready, willing, and able" to demonstrate the institutional values and virtues we extol.

Every generation has its own defining characteristics. Today's youth are characterized by increased interest and energy in assisting the less fortunate in our society. In many of our Lasallian institutions, there is extensive outreach into the local community. Students work hundreds of hours assisting the poor and needy. The degree to which we care for the least among us is the degree to which a society can consider itself socially conscious.

In many of our institutions, academic understandings are linked to action in the local community. Criminal justice departments work with street children; business departments sponsor training cooperatives for the poor; law students provide free services for the indigent; medical students visit the infirm elderly. Increasingly, these kinds of activities demonstrate that academic understandings have an important praxis with the world around us. They teach our students that education confers a *noblesse oblige* to care for others.

A heartening direction increasingly seen among our tertiary institutions is the engagement of adult populations of learners. With average life expectancy increasing dramatically in many of the developed countries, an able and skilled workforce may extend itself into years previously marked by retirement or diminished capacity. Lasallian universities are reaching out to these populations and providing them with new opportunities for training and education. The concept of "lifelong learning" is becoming internationally popular, and Lasallian institutions are in a good position to reach out to this otherwise marginalized adult population to provide enrichment programs, workforce training, diploma completion, and graduate work.

Lasallian institutions can engage adult learners so effectively because they already are predisposed to address the needs of marginal populations and have a clear understanding of "appropriate pedagogies." Adults learn differently than youth. Therefore, unique pedagogies are being implemented because, clearly, a traditional undergraduate curriculum is a poor fit for most adults. Using De La Salle's innovative spirit, global opportunities for adult learning are continually developing within the Lasallian system.

We are already seeing shifts in the way our students attend school. With increasing costs, students are working more and more hours to finance their higher educational degree. In some cases, this amounts to almost two full-time commitments. Students who, understandably, cannot handle this challenge may need to reduce their course load temporarily, step out of the educational track for a while, or extend their studies an extra year or two. Responsive to the social demands on our students, Lasallian institutions must exhibit flexibility in accommodating these working students. Supporting them through outreach services may be important in order to ensure completion of their degree. Indeed, without such credentials, they can become marginalized in our society. Accommodating their needs manifests our social consciousness to care for the disenfranchised.

3. Continuing Faithfulness to Innovation

One of the most enduring aspects of Lasallian education has been its capacity for innovation. Around the world, Lasallian colleagues creatively address educational issues of the moment in a manner rivaling fine artists masterfully brushing their canvasses. Understanding the realities of the moment, and appreciating the constraints under which they operate, our schools have achieved extraordinary success in addressing the diverse educational needs of people around the world.

Increasing size, stature, and recognition generally follow success. Such accomplishments are strong testimony to the good work that is being accomplished at the institution and serve to validate the public's endorsement of the enterprise. Increasing size can also cause institutions to be more cumbersome in responding to the signs of the time. Additional bureaucratic levels, necessitated by this change in enrollment, often can be slow, if not resistant, to innovation. Under such conditions, the very life-giving force that created the institution—innovation—can be threatened.

This seems paradoxical because better established institutions have amplified resources. They have worked for years to establish institutional largesse in support of their operations, often securing reserves for just such entrepreneurial ventures. Notwithstanding, higher educational institutions have inherent structures that contribute both to organizational stasis and to reduced capacity for welcoming fresh approaches or novel designs. This scenario is the stuff of which stereotypes are generated, as old, yellowed teaching plans resurface for yet another miraculous year of resuscitated instruction. New ideas and fresh programs are squelched under the rubric that "we have always done things this way," and creative programs, offerings, and departments are unable to be financed because "sacred cows," despite their limited usefulness, continue to graze heavily on precious budgets. Because of this, entrenched large educational institutions, which are otherwise considered successful, rarely earn the moniker of being educationally "fleet of foot."

In a rapidly changing global world (more to say about this later), it will be important to maintain De La Salle's spirit of innovation in education. In an increasingly mobile world, education is likely to be offered in a variety of venues, at a variety of times, to a variety of learners, at a variety of locations. Competition will challenge our institutions in the future; those that are not diversified and fail to engage innovative pathways may find themselves *in extremis*.

Fortunately, as a group, Lasallian institutions of higher education have many creative programs around the world that are serving individuals in remarkable ways. Occasions need to be found to borrow creative ideas from our sister institutions so that we can implement them on our own campuses. Meetings such as the IALU Cuernavaca conferences provide just such settings for the rich exchange of good ideas and best practices.

4. Retaining Our Institutional Uniqueness

Educational institutions are in an arms race. When a neighboring competitive institution adds a resource, constructs a new building, creates new scholarships, develops additional recreational facilities, or attracts a key professor, our institution feels the pressure to act similarly. Considering that prospective students increasingly weigh such factors in selecting schools, how administrators address these challenges from competing universities may be critical in positioning their own institution. Slowly, the position—and viability—of one's institution vis-à-vis other colleges is incrementally adjusted through each such administrative decision.

In responding to these challenges, there is a tendency for us to attempt to match such improvements one-for-one. Such actions, while improving the institution, can also impede the way in which we advance our mission. Should we use new funds to build a library or to offer enhanced student tuition support? Should we put money into recreational athletics instead of augmenting a struggling academic department's budget? If we establish equity by spreading available monies around so as to be relatively strong in most areas and distinctively good in none, does this advance the reputation of the institution?

In the years ahead, we will need to be very clear about the mission of our institutions. In doing so, we may need to become countercultural to some of the educational trends that would call us back into alignment with the pack. We need to selectively resist the pressures to look and act like so many other institutions. It will be important for us to retain our uniqueness and establish our own ground rules for measuring one institution against another. De La Salle's educational vision went well beyond establishing "just another school" for boys. He was creative, controversial, innovative, and entrepreneurial. The result was a unique educational perspective that has endured for more than three hundred years. That kind of uniqueness constantly recreates itself; and the result is a rebirth of the spirit that makes us so Lasallian.

Notwithstanding, there are strong forces that tempt us to conform to what others are doing and to be increasingly like them in many ways. An example of this is accreditation, which might serve as a good case study for the points I have been trying to make above.

Over time there has been a growth in the number of accrediting bodies whose approvals are highly sought. Instead of being used for constructive institutional reform, accreditation approval is often heralded as an institutional trophy. Indeed, multiple accreditations—often quite institutionally costly to obtain—promote an academic beauty contest mentality. The university with the most accreditations wins.

Accreditations guarantee that universities within a system have similar quality academic offerings. This facilitates credit transfers and helps to ensure a constant and upward quality of academic instruction. But accreditations can also have downsides.

In some cases, an institution may have to change its direction slightly (admit more males, reduce the teaching load of faculty, demand focused academic research) in order to comply with approval standards. While one accrediting institution's demands on a school may not be too onerous, over time, multiple accrediting institutions can place significant demands on an institution, actually causing it to move in a particular direction that might conflict with its core mission.

Accrediting institutions often use boilerplates to judge universities. Placing a boilerplate over the operations of a university and asking the university to "fit" the model causes universities to look the same over time (a statistical concept called "movement toward the mean"). To suggest that all higher educational institutions (including Lasallian schools) work toward being the same would be a terrible mistake. This action runs counter to a principle of diversity that confers strength on the American educational system. In the United States, heterogeneity enormously strengthens the mix of offerings within the educational academy.

This being said, there is need for us to work together and increasingly identify ourselves as Lasallian institutions. Branding our university as "Lasallian" helps all of our institutions to strengthen themselves through association. The Universidad La Salle system in Mexico has very effectively employed this strategy over the past decade. Each of its fourteen universities helps to reinforce the other by means of the same logo, colors, and name. In light of increased competition for students from governmental, private, and proprietary universities, it is helpful to have a common brand that emphasizes our unique education. When a student strolls down the street wearing a "Universidad La Salle" shirt, he is walking advertisement for all fourteen schools throughout Mexico!

5. Leveraging the Kinetics of Globalization

There is no doubt that globalization (the flow of goods, information, capital, and people across economic and political boundaries) is having an accelerating impact on higher education. Although globalization in and of itself is value neutral, it is widening gaps between developed and undeveloped countries, the effects of which—depending on one's location—can be beneficial or deleterious.

Business outsourcing and trade liberalization have brought countries into partnerships with unanticipated frequency. International labor migration and political pressure have also helped to drive globalization. Through Internet technologies, information flow has created a "digital divide" between those areas that have access and those that do not.

Globalization has helped to drive a number of positive improvements in education, but the benefits will not be uniformly recognized. These include, but are not limited to student exchanges, faculty collaborations, interinstitutional dialogue, joint degree programs, and enhanced sensitivity to cultural differences.

Within the Lasallian network, increased communication has taken place between institutions that were formerly isolated. The International Association of Lasallian Universities (IALU) has sponsored beneficial conferences each year to provide interinstitutional communication on a number of themes (including one on globalization!) that have helped all of our schools leverage the positive aspects of increased globalization. The publication of this collection of essays currently in your hands is evidence of increased cooperation among previously isolated Lasallian tertiary institutions around the world.

Because globalization has caused information to be a more valued commodity, there will be increased interest in obtaining a degree. In the future, individuals who hold advanced university degrees will be able to improve their lot in life, advancing themselves in society. As the world continues to develop, knowledge will become power: people with tertiary education degrees will distance themselves (economically and socially) from those without such degrees.

Because of the accelerating pace of globalization and the inherent educational divides it produces, Lasallian schools will need to work even harder to ensure fraternal collaboration. In some cases, this may require altruistic resource allocation and a re-establishment of one's priorities to include institutions other than one's own.

Increasingly, we are called upon to "think globally and act locally" in how we utilize resources. In a world of increasingly disparate finances and limited resources, we will need to both "think globally and act globally." As institutions that understand the ethical consequences of our actions, Lasallian institutions must teach students to consider thoughtfully the moral mortgage of globalization and act in a way that is consonant with one's ethical compass.

Institutionally, globalization demands that our structures be made more limber, more adaptable to people who are quickly changing their economic and social position, and more responsive to those who need our education. We cannot merely "ramp up" processes and procedures, but rather we need to be innovative in creating new programs to address the needs of individuals disenfranchised by globalization.

Two Challenges

There are a number of common challenges for Lasallian institutions in the years ahead. Two major challenges our institutions will see include how our institutions address accessibility and their relationship with the Roman Catholic Church.

Increasingly, our institutions will be pressured to maintain pristine facilities, support competitive salaries, provide contemporary equipment, and otherwise keep up with other more heavily funded institutions. As most of the funding for our institutions comes from tuition (with varying degrees of governmental and private support), there will be a tendency to increase per-student fees. We must be cautious about such increases. In augmenting tuitions, we incrementally begin to distance ourselves from those we wish to serve. Even in cases where support for low-income students can be leveraged with income from full-pay students, the desired number of low-pay students often cannot be completely accommodated. Low-income students may not even consider attendance at such schools. Indeed, even students in the middle of the socioeconomic ladder may be deleteriously impacted.

Secondly, our institutions will come under increasing pressure to define very concretely their relationship with the Roman Catholic Church. The United States is experiencing heightened interest in the juridical implications of *Ex Corde Ecclesiae* as institutions struggle to determine their appropriate relationship with local Ordinaries. In some areas, disenfranchisement with the Church has caused a shift from the parish to the college or university as the loci for religious activity. In responding to this trend, universities will need to examine the sufficiency of their provisions for spiritual exercises, social praxis, and theological enrichment.

Epilogue

This essay suggests that we will meet some challenges and wonderful opportunities as we move forward. Knowing the breadth and depth of our Lasallian system, I am certain that we will meet those moments with unprecedented success. Increasingly, Lasallian universities will offer a special kind of education: one which is faithful to the values espoused by our Founder and one that is cherished by all who have been its beneficiary.

Every day I give thanks for the opportunity to work in a system that does so very much for so very many. Around the world, talented, dedicated, and extremely capable people perform daily miracles by educationally transforming students. Perhaps Penelope's line from Stephen Phillips' *Ulysses* speaks best to explain the success of our enterprise: we have been "true to a vision, steadfast to a dream." I am proud and honored to be part of an enterprise that has such a rich history and a hopeful future.

Author Biography

Br. Craig Franz is president of Saint Mary's University of Minnesota and president emeritus of Saint Mary's College of California (USA). Founder of the International Association of Lasallian Universities, he has served as president since 1997. A former Fulbright Senior Fellow, Brother Craig has published extensively in his own academic field of marine ecology as well as in his professional area of higher educational administration.

Appendix

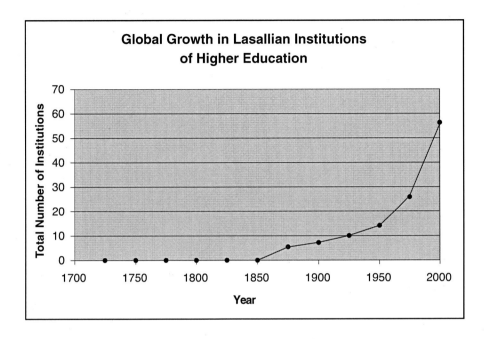

THE LASALLIAN UNIVERSITY

By: Br. Edgard Hengemüle, FSC

Lasallian Inspiration

Our universities are Lasallian. This means that they are inspired by De La Salle.

But as it happens, practically the only experience De La Salle had regarding the university was the one he had as a university student. The educational practice to which he devoted himself afterward, and the reflections he developed as a result, were not situated in higher education, but in elementary education.

Why, then, if neither his practice nor his theoretical developments are relative to the university world, can he, today, inspire the Lasallians who work in that world?

He can inspire us, first of all, by the example he set for us. He was not content to stay with only his seminary education, but took university courses suitable to his vocational choice, going through all its degrees, from the lowest degree to the highest—and all that not without serious impediments along the way. He can also inspire us by the character that he gave to his educational work and to the way he accomplished it.

De La Salle as a University Student

First, De La Salle can inspire us by his example, by the appreciation he demonstrated for the university studies he undertook.

After his early education, begun within his family, in October 1661, he started studying in the college of the University of Reims. Between 1661 and 1664, he took courses from the sixth to the third class, studying especially Latin and Greek. In 1665, in the second class, he took humanities, and in 1666, the first, rhetoric. The school periods of 1667 and 1668 were dedicated to philosophy. This cycle of studies was crowned with the title master of arts, or master of philosophy, qualifying *summa cum laude*, which allowed him, thenceforth, to teach in colleges. In 1669, still in Reims, he started the course of theology, which he continued, from 1670 on, in Paris, more precisely at the Sorbonne.

In April 1672, when his father passed away, De La Salle had to go back to Reims and continue his studies in his hometown. In August he concluded the three years of theology, which took him to the baccalaureate of that university. Then, until September 1673, he interrupted his studies because of the time consumed by his new position as substitute-head of his family.

To graduate with the title bachelor of theology, the statutes of the University of Reims required two more years of scholastic philosophy as a complement to the knowledge acquired in this area before the acquisition of the title master of arts. So between October 1673 and August 1675, De La Salle took those two complementary years of philosophy, after which he received the title bachelor of theology that he had been working for.

Between 1675 and the beginning of 1678, he prepared his undergraduate degree in theology. Between October and December 1675, with an eye on admission to that degree, he asked for the designation of three doctors to examine his competence in positive theology, scholastic theology, sacraments, history of the Church, and sacred Scripture. He took the selection exam and was approved. In the two years of preparation for the undergraduate degree, in addition to classes taught by doctors, what he had to do was perform his personal studies, participate in the defense of theses, and present theses of his own. Having accomplished those requirements, he obtained the undergraduate degree in theology in January 1678, which qualified him to teach that subject.

Between February 1678 and Easter of 1680, he interrupted studies and thesis defenses because in that time important events took place that determined his future: his ordination in April 1678; then, weeks later, Roland's death and the known consequences this had on his life; in March 1679, the arrival in Reims of Professor Nyel, an event that triggered others—also known to us but totally unforeseen.

After this, having complied with all the necessary requirements, he crowned his career as a university student with the title doctor of theology, attained in 1680.

Faith, Fraternity, and Service

Second, we said, De La Salle can inspire us by the characterization that he gave to his educational work and to his way of accomplishing it.

We can observe this characterization, for example, in the educational practices developed in his institutions, as well as in the type of relationship among the people who carry them out, and in the mystique that inspires them.

For him, the religious Brothers, whose order he founded, carry out an educational mission, accomplished in a community, as an expression of their consecration to God: consecration, mission, community.

Today, it is common to say, always more often and in more places, that all the Lasallians, including those who act at the university level, find inspiration in their Founder and express their faith through an educational service accomplished in fraternity: faith, fraternity, service.

Faith

The university that De La Salle attended kept the religious traces of the origin of this institution alive. Likewise, the schools that he created were

"Christian schools." He conceived them and made them work as pastoral tools, as places to launch the foundations of the Church, to provide Christian education, to form true Christians.

Our universities will be Lasallian, first of all, insofar as they keep this original characteristic of the university in general and of the Lasallian educational work in particular.

Generally speaking, our universities have to guarantee a Christian presence in higher education. They must maintain a dialoguing mediation between the Church and the different areas of the cultural world, to be the voice of the Church to talk to this world, but also to be the ears of the Church, to listen to what this world has to tell her. They are entitled to contribute to the creation of a synthesis of faith, culture, and life; to help illuminate questions raised by science and technology; and, with the results of their research placed at our disposal, to help answer current problems and meet challenges.

For this to be so, in practical terms, we must think of our universities as Catholic, and present them transparently as such. We should inform people clearly about their identity and about the consequences that derive from them; make their identity present in our official positions and decisions; respect the religious options of the members of the institution, but also require respect for our own confessional option. We must be in communion with the Church—on the one hand, to believe in the propedeutic value that an authentic humanization has for faith, to believe that an openness to the truth disposes to an adherence to the total Truth; and, on the other hand, not to fail to explicitly propose the person and the message of Jesus Christ, as well as that of the Church, especially its ethic and social doctrine, and to offer opportunities to the ones who want them so that they can grow in the faith and bear witness to it. And, finally, so that all this might become a reality, especially so that the theological illumination and the Christian orientation may be guaranteed, the functioning of an organized and dynamic pastoral service is indispensable.

Fraternity

It is quite well known how the community dimension, constitutive of nascent universities, is also fundamental for De La Salle and his cofounders. De La Salle did not form isolated teachers, "mavericks" in education. He constituted them in a magisterial body. He made them reflect and act "together and by association." And this united reflection and action was one of the roots of the success of the Lasallian educational work from its beginnings.

What is pertinent to this characterization of his schools is that De La Salle wanted them to be laboratories of human acquaintanceship and Christian fraternity, by the relationship of the teachers among themselves as well as the teachers with their pupils, and of the pupils among themselves.

One of the reasons why students choose Lasallian universities should be the fraternal environment, the attention to the people, the respect for the differences reigning among them. They must constitute academic communities. In them the "together by association" must be upgraded to a university style, that is to say, by a joint action of a human group dedicated to research, to teaching and learning, and to service for society; by a common consecration [devotion] to the search for truth; by the sharing of ideas and ideals; and by planning, accomplishment, and collective evaluation of activities.

As institutions of an international Institute, our universities must always continue implementing the "together and by association" on a global scale, by the definition of a common identity, always respectful of the local peculiarities, by a joint reflection, by the circulation of information, by the exchange of people, and by the cooperation in common research and action projects in their specific field.

Service

Since its origins, the university constitutes itself as an agency rendering services to people, to the Church, to the State, and to society in general.

As far as De La Salle himself is concerned, it is well known which service he rendered as a response to the necessities and aspirations of his times, namely, the "Christian school." And he never fails to repeat for whom he wanted his educational service to be: the children, and all of them, since God wants all of them, as well as all the people, "to come to the knowledge of the truth" (MTR 193.1). Neither is it necessary to remind us to whom he rendered primarily his educative service—to the children of "the artisans and the poor." What may perhaps be appropriate to remember is his wish that such service be a service centered in the person of the pupil, considered, in his school, as the real lord, for whose benefit the teacher should employ all of his time and efforts—as a servant must employ all of his time in favor of his master (MF 92.3).

For our reflection, it is also important to keep in mind how much De La Salle wanted the educational service that he offered to be (although in his time he would not have used these words) one of an integral and integrating kind, and for him, integral education also included the professional dimension.

His concern for integral education, as he expresses it, is embodied synthetically in the words, "teaching to live well" (CR I.3). He accomplishes it by seeing to it that his pupils be formed as much at the physical level as at the psychic and spiritual; by offering them simultaneously—in Blain's expression (p. 350), "instruction (religious) and education," that is to say, profane culture and evangelization—by seeing to it that his schools prepare them, at the same time, to be true Christians and good citizens (MF 160.3). And for him, what makes an integrated education is faith. Faith unifies, in a single unique glance, all the knowledge and all learned undertakings, and gives them transcendental meaning and direction.

The subject of professional preparation, included in an integral education, is linked to another question that is strongly present in De La Salle, and that is his endeavor to offer an education embedded in daily living. An education that, first of all, comes from life and is an answer to concrete needs, as was the need to keep children away from idleness and its "disastrous consequences" (CRI.6; MTR 194.1), or the need to educate difficult youngsters, or even re-educate delinquents. And, secondly, an education that prepares for life: life in general and Christian and professional life in particular.

The employability of the pupil was clearly a part of De La Salle's concerns. For him, children also come to school so that they may be "in a condition to be employed when their parents want them to go to work" (MTR, 194.1). Especially if the candidate for the Lasallian school is older, the school that receives him must be informed by the parents about "what they want for him, if they want him to learn a craft and in how much time" (CE, p. 250), and this, evidently, so that the school may know and may prioritize, in the pupil's curriculum, what is more useful for his future employment. And, generally speaking, De La Salle is aware that what an artisan's son learns in his school allows him to be, in the context of time, "capable of everything" (CE, p. 187).

In concrete terms, professional formation in his institutions was double: direct and indirect, explicit and implicit, focused and comprehensive. A school like the Sunday school provided some elements of direct professional formation to young laborers. Both the Novitiate and the Seminary for Rural Teachers prepared professionals explicitly to work in classrooms. But, in a broad sense, his elementary "Christian school" also prepared for employment, providing the pupil with resources useful in any job context, such as reading, writing, and calculating, and developing in him dispositions, attitudes, and habits of life appreciated in any professional situation, such as a liking for work, the capability and the practice of accomplishing it in an orderly and efficient way, the assiduity or punctuality in showing up for work, or ethics in the relationships established therein.

It is also necessary not to forget how much De La Salle wants his educational service to be efficient, that his school "goes on well" (*Letters* 34.18; 57.12; 58.20; 75.8 . . .), that real learning and human and Christian formation can take place there. So that this may happen, he takes care that the contents be adequate, even advanced for his time, and sequentially kept in order; that the methods considered best for his time be used; that a proper environment for schoolwork be created; that time be integrally utilized; that assiduity and punctuality be guaranteed; and that the promotion of the pupils be undertaken seriously. If necessary, he uses correction for the pupils who are not diligent with their school duties. But he also knows how to stimulate those who are assiduous and highly interested in the study with rewards. He guarantees strong unity, even uniformity in the organization and implementation of the teaching, without impeding personal creativity, only requiring that its consonance with the Lasallian style of teaching be submitted to the discernment of the superior. At an operational level, he ensures the careful management and administration of his schools. In the same way, he does not tolerate that external interferences disturb the administrative and pedagogic autonomy that he demands in order to accomplish his method of education. And, above all, he bases the quality of his teaching and education on his staff of teachers, conscious of the greatness and responsibility of their mission, prepared to accomplish it ("your ignorance would be criminal": MF 153.1). These are teachers who produce pedagogical knowledge, surely "made by experience" (as Paulo Freire would say, in the twentieth century), but also a product of the exchange of ideas (the "Guía" tells about the *"beaucoup de conférences"*), and who transmit this accumulated knowledge to the younger teachers who follow them.

To this, finally, it should be added that De La Salle does not want his school to be an island, but to be open to the Church community and to the civil environment in which it is established, and, most of all, to the families it serves through education, in order to render a better service.

Projecting to the present day the directions set forth by De La Salle, and adding to them orientations and practices that he could not foresee, it seems to be important that in our program for higher education, we have a certain consensus in the sense that

- as a university in general, we will be a center for the preservation, the production, and the diffusion of knowledge of all nature, and as a Catholic and Lasallian university, we will particularly be attentive to the preservation, the production, and the diffusion of theoretic and practical knowledge related to education and pedagogy, and to theology and pastoral ministry.

- we will have as reference the person of the young people and adults who attend it. We will treat them as such as a whole, and each one in particular.

- insofar as Lasallian education is aimed preferably at the poor and the necessity and aspiration for higher education increases, we will persevere in a creative search for the means to make this teaching accessible to those who cannot afford it from their own resources.

- we will contribute to the promotion of the human person and to overcoming poverty and social injustice by studying the roots of poverty and of injustice with our students, promoting in them social awareness and commitment.

- following the line of an education that comes from life and prepares for it, we will form professionals who are able to respond to the needs of today's world with realism and competence.

- in a world of knowledge progressively more fragmented by modernity and by specialization taken to the extreme, a world where universal knowledge is no longer possible, we will establish, at least, links between knowledge, and will promote interdisciplinary dialogues on the major issues that affect people and the world as a whole.

- aware of the eminently professional purpose of university teaching, we will take great pains to avoid "sterile academicism." But, at the same time, we will take care lest we fall into "immediatist productivism" (Delors, p. 142). In the university, we will also continue to be attentive to people's global maturing, to their human and spiritual growth; to their development as persons of eminent knowledge, but also as emotionally balanced individuals capable of creative and responsible action. We will help them propose a life-project broader than a professional one, to opt for a philosophy of life, to build a sense of life that is transcendental for the concepts learned and of the techniques mastered.

- we will stand for academic excellence. And we will do this with updated programs, efficient and scientifically founded methodologies, the use of available technology, the guarantee of the necessary material infrastructure, rigorous evaluations, efficient management, the defense of our institutional autonomy, the guarantee of academic freedom, and, most of all, the competence of our professors.

- we will keep our university connected to its religious, cultural, social, and economic environment. We will keep it open, dialoguing, and available to society and its organizations as a whole. Concretely, we will have it help to detect local and regional needs, to convert them into research subjects, and to offer clues to resolve them. And we will carry out integrated and cooperative two-way work with our environment: on the one hand, we will make sure our university is at its service by applying to it its researched knowledge; on the other hand, we will expect and request our environment's collaboration, such as company internships for university students and the availability of professionals who would like to share with them their ideas and experiences.

- at the same time, while keeping our feet very firmly on local ground, we will keep our eyes open and raised to universal realities, remembering that we are preparing "university" students for an increasingly more globalized world, and that we are pedagogic and spiritual disciples of someone who dreamed of our expanding the glory of God, through education, "all over the world" (SM 46.3).

- we will always keep in mind that this whole project of the Lasallian university will not be accomplished if it does not go through the professors, and that it will go through them only if they are offered initial and continued formation in the ideals and in the practice of Lasallian education.

Author Biography

Br. Edgard Hengemüle has served as the coordinator for the Department of Pedagogy and Campus Ministry for the District of Porto Alegre, Brazil. A former Visitor of the Lasallian District of Porto Alegre, Brazil, he has also served as president and executive secretary for the Lasallian Latin American Region. A professor of the history of education, he has written widely on Saint John Baptist de La Salle.

Bibliography

Blain, Jean-Baptiste. La vie de Monsieur Jean-Baptiste de La Salle. V. II. Rouen : Jean-Baptiste Machuel, 1733.

Delors, Jacques. Educação, um tesouro a descobrir. 3 ed. São Paulo: Cortez; Brasília: MEC; UNIESCO, 1999.

Félix, Paul. Las cartas de San Juan Bautista de La Salle (Cartas). Traducción de la edición francesa, adaptada y editada por el Instituto Pontificio San Pio X. Madrid: Juan Bravo, 1962.

La Salle, Jean-Baptiste de. Conduite des Écoles chrétiennes (CE). Rome: Maison Saint Jean-Baptiste de La Salle, 1965.

———. Méditations sur les principales fêtes de l'anée (MTR). Rouen: J-B. Machuel, 1731.

———. Règles Communes des Frères des Écoles Chrétiennes (RC). Rome: Maison Saint Jean-Baptiste de La Salle, 1965.

LASALLIAN HIGHER EDUCATION: A QUEST FILLED WITH PARADOXICAL AND AMBIGUOUS SHADES OF REALITY

By: Br. Louis DeThomasis, FSC

Education is the reshaping of life's forms
with end (meaning) but without end (termination).
—Gabriel Moran

Introduction

In his 1987 book, *No Ladder to the Sky: Education and Morality*, former Christian Brother and the director of the religious education program at New York University, Gabriel Moran, presented an engaging paradox. The paradox was created by his double meaning for the word *end*. He posited that the human impulse to reach an end (termination) makes it difficult to conceive of education as lifelong. With his distinctive creativity, Moran argued that if *end* as meaning can be distinguished from *end* as termination, then we can talk of ends in an endless process. He concluded that we cannot have an adequate meaning of education unless these two different meanings of *end* are kept in tension with each other.

I am convinced that if we modern-day Lasallians are to be a vital and relevant factor in higher education in the future, and if we intend to be an effective force for addressing real-world, global issues of social injustice, we must embrace the same type of tension exposed by Moran. However, inasmuch as almost three decades have passed since he authored his book, in today's world we must embrace different and diverse types of contemporary ambiguities. If we become complacent in our work and fail to develop an understanding of these modern-day paradoxes, we will lose the unique dynamism and genius of the Lasallian charism.

We must remember that in the seventeenth century, there was an acute and dire need for a revolution in educational practices. De La Salle imagined and then implemented a creative transformation that empowered education to reshape the lives of his needy students with an end (meaning) in mind, but without end (termination) to its pedagogical possibilities. De La Salle acted upon the classic Latin understanding of education, *ex ducare* (to lead *from* or *beyond*), instead of what was then the prevailing teaching paradigm of a tutor leading a student *to* a set, predetermined, static state. The Christian message of love, hope, and compassion imbued De La Salle's pedagogy and provided an essential and intrinsic component of his education model without "end" (termination), setting the stage for the Lasallian charism to be necessarily and intentionally an "endless process."

With the benefit of hindsight and contemporary concepts, it may not be difficult for us to promote understanding that in the charism of De La Salle, education changed from a journey of teaching to a quest for learning. Granted we usually do not describe his contributions to education in these terms. But underscoring the centrality of the quest for learning serves to remind our modern-day Lasallians in higher education of the following:

- The revolution De La Salle launched continues.

- We, too, are called to be "revolutionaries."

- We, too, are compelled to have the faith and zeal to prudently discard past solutions that are no longer effective in today's global society.

- We, too, must be willing to embrace anew the Lasallian charism: not as an "end" (termination), but rather as an "end" (new meaning), by committing to be even more adamantly practical and more brilliantly creative than Saint John Baptist de La Salle himself!

Those committed to Lasallian higher education should consider three areas within today's global milieu that can be formative in our quest to seek current opportunities and envision future possibilities for revitalizing the Lasallian charism in the third millennium. Each area, however, presents paradoxical and/or ambiguous shades of reality since, as Moran has so eloquently observed, "Education is the reshaping of life's forms with end (meaning) but without end (termination)."

A Different Commitment to Social Responsibility

The familiar and essential concepts of social justice, social awareness, and social responsibility "trigger" good Lasallian educators to "target" their educational aims and goals toward improving the lives of the poor, the marginalized, and the oppressed. We receive this vision, of course, from the meaning (end) offered to us in De La Salle's charism to teach the poor. However, I fear that we Lasallians have come to look upon De La Salle's goal to teach the poor as an "end" in itself (termination), without embracing sufficiently today's increasingly complex global reality— a reality totally and incommensurably different from De La Salle's times. As I indicated in a previous paper, *Lasallian Higher Education: Coloring Outside the Lines*, De La Salle's creative and innovative educational approaches focused on the educational needs of the individual. As a result, he successfully and effectively advanced the cause of social justice for both the "haves" and the "have nots" of his times.

Yet, today, even as ever more educational opportunities are made available to unprecedented numbers of people, we see in our global society expansion of the ugly and intolerable presence of poverty. And we find this poverty not only where it might be expected, in the third world and developing areas on our globe, but also in developed and more prosperous countries where social injustice is manifest in a burgeoning class of people called the "working poor."

Our mandate in Lasallian higher education today is to understand and appreciate De La Salle's charism to teach the poor directly in a new and different light, because the traditional end (meaning) is not sufficient for today's world. Despite the anxiety and fear that may accompany its articulation, we must heed a call to "re-imagine" anew, without end (termination), the Lasallian charism. In today's global society, it is no longer *enough* to teach the poor directly, however ennobling that is. I do not suggest we should not teach the poor directly; rather, I underscore that teaching the poor exclusively is no longer sufficient. Let me explain.

The vast and complex network that comprises the global economy clutches a majority of the citizens of this planet with a new "invisible hand." Unlike the more benign "invisible hand" of Adam Smith, today's invisible hand plunges people deep into an infrastructure of a poverty that involves our core values, our cultures, our economic institutions, and our governments. So insidious is this reality that former U.S. Secretary of Labor Robert B. Reich observes in his book *I'll Be Short: Essentials for a Decent Working Society* that unbridled global capital is undermining any social contract among people and governments and industry. But he also points out that we must not be passive victims of such economic forces.

We must understand, therefore, that the problem is systemic. Consequently, any viable solution to social injustice and poverty must also be systemic. Therein lay new challenges and opportunities for Lasallian higher education. Our Lasallian charism must propel us to create a new educational infrastructure that extends beyond the educational needs of the poor (i.e., "direct service to the poor") and fosters a systemic change in all of Lasallian higher education that addresses the very core of societal structures, systems and dynamics.

The Lasallian vision for third-millennium higher education should compel us to create anew an innovative infrastructure in which our faculties, our research, and our curricula empower us not only to teach the poor directly but also to help our students (even our most advantaged) learn and possess the "tools" to change both the world and the systemic and structural forces that create the poor within that world.

If we continue to look upon our Lasallian charism as an "end" and limit ourselves to teaching the poor directly, then all we accomplish is to help certain poor individuals out of poverty; but then we unintentionally send them forth into a chronically and structurally unjust society. No, of course, this is not what any of us desire. Our Lasallian charism must be reinvented, reinvigorated, and renewed!

I do not in any way suggest that we abandon our direct service to the poor. On the contrary, our call is to expand the scope of our vision through a newly created Lasallian higher education network that will enable us to prepare our students—the poor and the advantaged—for lives of service and leadership that will effectively influence our societies to a new practical and ethical social order. Lasallian universities cannot be passive victims to social and economic demands; rather we must study, research and demonstrate to our students how we and they can transform our societies into socially responsible free enterprise systems.

We "re-invent" our Lasallian charism by "re-imagining" the genius of De La Salle into a new vision for Lasallian higher education. The goal of replacing the grave issues and burdens of the poor and vulnerable in our global society with a just social order requires more than fervent and repeated exhortation of our Church's magnificent and value-based "preferential option for the poor." That alone is not enough!

The transformation can only be accomplished if Lasallian higher education leaders think and lead globally. Armed with our Lasallian charism, we must no longer view ourselves as individual Lasallian institutions of higher learning. We must envision a new Lasallian higher education network that effectively interweaves our sensitivity to God's plan for peace and justice for all humankind: a Lasallian ethical global-learning community. Our Lasallian charism can enjoy a new awakening as we unfold an innovative network of creative, flexible, adaptive, and fluid strategic alliances and partnerships. Consider the keen insight of Gareth Morgan in his book *Images of Organization*: "Images and metaphors are not only interpretive constructs or ways of seeing; they also provide frameworks for action. Their use creates insights that often allow us to act in ways that we may not have thought possible."

Concisely stated, the vision for Lasallian higher education at this beginning of the third millennium is to prepare its students to create and shape a new, just global society—not just to facilitate access for the poor and needy to education—and then to fix a world order that is "broken."

A Different Commitment to Religion

Continuing this reflection and looking at possible future visions that will affect our Lasallian higher education opportunities, I suggest we consider perhaps the most problematic area for us: religion. Continuing the themes of "paradox" and "ambiguity," religion is one of the more difficult conundrums we are presented with in Catholic higher education today worldwide. Religion (i.e., our Catholic faith) is a core and central component in the life of Lasallian higher educational institutions. Truly it is the essence of the spirit of our Lasallian charism. Yet, as paradoxical as it may seem on our ever shrinking globe today, religions—particularly dogmatic and doctrinal ideologies—are at the core and center of prevalent global distrust, hatred, and terrorism. Quite a distressing paradox! Using Moran's paradox once again may help us comprehend this terrible "praxis." For many, and in frighteningly growing numbers, religion as an "end" (termination) of further discussion and exploration has surpassed religion as an "end" (meaning) to express more expansive and newly gained insights into the message of love found in all world religions.

Whether the topic is human life, economic life, culture, education, or religion, we should understand ideology as a systematic body of concepts, integrated assertions, and theories that constitute a view of reality. For intellectuals, ideology has held a powerful and influential appeal that can be traced back to the efforts of the French "Enlightenment," which produced a set of "mechanical laws" to explain human nature. Today's ideologues, irrespective of country, culture, or religion, share with the proponents of the Enlightenment this mechanistic, rigid style of thinking. Kenneth Minogue, in his book *Alien Powers: The Pure Theory of Ideology*, warns of the ideologue's tendency to consistently lean toward certainty (i.e., "my" certainty). Minogue convincingly places ideology in the perspective of a perversion of reason. In essence, ideology is to reason as gluttony is to fine dining! The grave danger inherent in any ideology, some say, is its propensity to become an intellectual chameleon, since it appears sometimes as a science, other times as a philosophy, or oftentimes and most dangerously as a religion. Religious ideology becomes an insidious enemy for Lasallian higher education, since it casts a shadow over the human imagination by offering neat ideological formulae under the guise of "total truth."

Let me emphasize that I am not pointing to religion as *the* problem, but rather to religious ideologies that prostitute the wholesome and good principles and values of Christianity and other world religions. Throughout history, religious ideologies have cast dark—and in some cases evil—shadows over our globe. By attesting to the so-called principles that emanate from their ideologies rather than from the basic truths of their religion, religious ideologues—even to this day—justify detestable acts of human travesty and terror. Relying on their perversion of reason, they seek to justify the ethics of their actions.

Ideologues of every persuasion contribute to this intellectual prostitution of principles and values. We live in an era in which indignation has become a way of life. Some conservatives are disposed to proclaim that everybody should "pay their own way." Some liberals ceaselessly promote a "Robin Hood-esque" economic system. Some academicians elevate "political correctness" to the highest priority. And some religious place all their hopes in the occurrence of some miraculous epiphany. Today, ideologues of all types abound and insist that adherence to their principles and beliefs offer the only opportunity for emerging from the shadows of destruction; but, instead, their fervor and their frenzy drive us deeper into the shackles of distrust and terror that inevitably change "education" into "indoctrination."

Even a superficial overview of current events highlights a strange phenomenon in the socioreligious realm. We can readily and easily observe both the expanding worldwide skepticism about organized religions (ideologue skeptics) and the concurrent growing worldwide movement toward religious fundamentalism (ideologue fundamentalists). Ideologue skeptics breed suspicion, distrust, and paranoia about organized religions, claiming that the core values of peace and human dignity promoted by established religions are to be despised and discarded as nothing more than futile plots that infringe on people's individual and personal freedoms. Rigid ideologue-fundamentalists take their suspicion, distrust, and paranoia to more outrageous (not higher, just more outrageous) levels, as they replace the core values of peace and human dignity of their own religions with cacophonous and rabid calls to strike down the infidels, kill the unbelievers, and terrorize everyone into submission to their vision of "God's will be done." Both the skeptics and the fundamentalists lead us to pose the question: How can the dynamics of global education be functional when ideologues, in the name of religion, take on the armor of secular power and increasingly resort to hostility and terror?

Simply stated, in our world today the great religions play a radically different role than most of us would like to believe. It is today's global tragedy that the ideologues within religions—rather than being part of the solution to our global conflicts—have been significant, contributing, and causal factors of the problems we face. The insidious perspectives promulgated by religious fundamentalist ideologues around the globe alienate peoples, nations, religions, cultures, and economies; and because they perpetuate environments of distrust, hatred, and instability, they make Lasallian higher education more difficult—but more necessary—than ever.

In this context Lasallian higher education has a golden opportunity to forge a new alliance between the sacred and the secular worlds, if only we find the courage to discard any pretensions to see the sacred and the secular as opposites, as competitors, and as mutually exclusive. The floodlight of history illumines countless examples of the unspeakable horrors and destructive tendencies of both worlds, especially when they are not tempered by the Lasallian charism of faith and zeal.

I believe it is essential for Lasallian higher education to address this current and growing paradox on our globe by embracing our Lasallian charism and challenging ourselves to educate our students with the "faith" of our Christian heritage; *but* also with a new "zeal," in which religion is a unifying force for good, for love, and for understanding among all on our shrinking globe. It is we Lasallians who must discover new ways to teach that our core Christian dynamic that "we may all be one" does not mean that we must all be the same!

A Different Commitment to Education

For more than three centuries, faith and zeal have been the distinguishing hallmarks of Lasallian educators. We see men and women who—to this day—continue to be pragmatic, effective, and dedicated to providing vibrant and relevant education for their students. However, as with all commitments, our language, our vocabulary, and our ideals need to be updated and reimagined in order that we not fall into the trap of complacency or the doldrums of the familiar to the extent that we develop boredom in our vocation as educators. I am reminded of the famous book about Savannah, Georgia, *Midnight in the Garden of Good and Evil*, in which a courtly, elderly gentleman walks around the city holding a dog leash, but there is no dog attached to it! And the people who pass him walking his "dog" greet him with, "Still walking the dog, Mr. Glover?"

We know that many who are familiar with Lasallian higher education throughout the world respect our dedication and commitment to De La Salle's charism. But I wonder—I fear—that perhaps, similar to Mr. Glover, we walk around the halls of academe without a clever, dynamic, and renewed vision of just what LaSallian higher education is in today's global society. Let me explain.

History provides ample evidence of the great influence the Church had on the intellectual formation of modern thought. Based on the great Greek philosophers and their emphasis on reason and logic, the Church developed an entire intellectual infrastructure. Even in the early days, the Church always placed enormous importance on the great God-given gift to humanity: reason. With only a cursory review of the great medieval

Church-sponsored universities and the teachings of the learned scholastics of that time, we can see how this commitment to the power of reason led to the development of science, to a liberation of people, and to a more democratic society. Of course, the Church continually guarded its deposit of faith as it pertained to its theological canons. But such "protectionism" did not significantly impede the macro-movement of Western civilization and its academic pursuits toward progress in the arts, the sciences, and the sociopolitical dynamics in the course of history since the so-called Dark Ages.

Can we be as confident today in our Catholic colleges and universities throughout the world that there remains a strong commitment to the primacy of reason, open dialogue, questioning spirit, and freedom to creatively explore "faith seeking reason"? Or more precisely, is the institutional Church encouraging us and providing us with an infusion of a spirit to progressively seek understanding of the diversity of humanity and a world coming together through modern technology as never before?

Given the increasing influence of fundamentalism in all world religions, including Christianity (as we discussed above), and given the expansive explosion of information and knowledge generated from ever-growing technologies, and given the vast pluralism and diversity of cultures and religions commingling on this shrinking globe, can we be assured of a strong, faith-filled commitment to our powers of reason and free intellectual pursuit in Catholic higher education?

I do not believe that anywhere in Catholic higher education on this globe today, any of us are exempt from real and pervasive tensions with our independence and autonomy to pursue knowledge through reason while still remaining faithful to our faith and revelation as taught by the Magisterium of the Church. In a world filled with a diversity of cultures and a pluralism of views, Catholic higher education does not have to succumb to a "dictatorship of relativism"; however, neither does it have to succumb to a "dictatorship of doctrinalism" that prohibits open and reasonable inquiry.

With much sensitivity and complete faithfulness to the Church, Lasallian higher education institutions today must demonstrate that we are not "Church"; rather we are "University." As such, though we remain faithful to the Church and assist the Church in its sacred role "to teach as Jesus did," Lasallian universities must be free, open, and reasonable venues for seeking ultimate truth in a different manner and style than the "Church." Truly, the "Word of God" is proclaimed, protected, and taught by the Church. The discussion and inquiry required because of the diverse cultures extant in our world compel us to unfold the meaningfulness of the "Word of God." With Catholic universities and their intellectual exploration with their students while utilizing the "full light of reason," Catholic universities assist the Church in this mission.

As I reflect on the future of Lasallian higher education, I see a distinctive and unequivocal need for us as Lasallian educators to have the fortitude to encourage and foster new understandings, new ideas, and new uncharted paths to our faith-filled commitment to the Gospel and the Church. It will take the courage, faith, and zeal of De La Salle's charism because, given the present milieu of Church governance, we risk misunderstanding and tension.

Lasallian higher education must take on a vision of faith-filled courage for it to be true to our Lasallian heritage:

- Courage—to be leaders unafraid to address the insidious problem caused by the religious ideologues around the globe and in the Church whose so-called religious doctrine alienates peoples, religions, and nations while perpetrating a milieu of hatred.

- Courage—to be Lasallian "spiritualists" who will guide our students to embrace and feel the love of Jesus, rather than just to be absorbed by ideological aspects of the Church.

- Courage—to be supporters of our students as they journey in *their* ways, with *their* language and *their* styles, to discover the faith that is in them.

Conclusion

In this brief presentation, I have attempted to cast some future vision about Lasallian higher education by approaching the need for a different commitment in three of our traditional areas of concern: social responsibility, religion, and education. Of course, there are many more areas that could be discussed and must eventually be addressed. However, in a certain sense, *how* we categorize the areas of concern is less relevant then *how* we come together in association to address our future as Lasallian higher education leaders. As I end this reflection, I remind you of the beginning insight of Gabriel Moran: "Education is the reshaping of life's forms with end (meaning) but without end (termination)."

Though this is an "end" to this reflection, I am firmly convinced that, as long as we are committed and faithful to our Lasallian charism to come together in association, there will never be an "end" to teaching minds and touching hearts.

Live, Jesus, in our hearts. Forever!

Author Biography

Br. Louis DeThomasis is the chancellor of Saint Mary's University of Minnesota (USA). With his broad business and investment knowledge, he was founder and chairman of Christian Brothers Investment Services, Inc., and currently serves as a director of the Galaxy Funds. Brother Louis has written extensively about the power of an ethical financial world as a dynamic for creating a better future for humanity.

Selected Bibliography

For further study of some of the ideas presented in this paper, see the following resources:

DeThomasis, Louis, FSC (2004). "Lasallian Higher Education: Coloring Outside the Lines." Paper presented at the meeting of the International Association of Lasallian Universities—Encuentro VII, Barcelona, Spain.

Jenkins, Philip (2002). *The Next Christendom: The Coming of Global Christianity*. New York: W. W. Norton and Company.

Johnson, Elizabeth A., CSJ (2003). *Truly Our Sister: A Theology of Mary in the Communion of Saints*. New York: Continuum.

Minogue, Kenneth (1985). *Alien Powers: The Pure Theory of Ideology*. New York: St. Martin's Press.

Moran, Gabriel (1987). *No Ladder to the Sky: Education and Morality*. San Francisco: Harper and Row.

Morgan, Gareth (1986). *Images of Organization*. Beverly Hills, CA: Sage Publications.

Reich, Robert B. (2002). *I'll Be Short: Essentials for a Decent Working Society*. Boston: Beacon Press.

Vogel, David (2005). *The Market for Virtue*. Washington, DC: Brookings Institute Press.

TRANSFORMATION AND INNOVATION IN LASALLIAN UNIVERSITIES

By: Juan Antonio Ojeda, FSC

Introduction

Like many other higher educational institutions, Lasallian universities are rife with internal and external controversies. It is a crucial moment for analysis, deep revision, and transformation. From all sides, higher education is being questioned and multiple solutions are being proposed. Individuals position themselves in very different ways when facing the change that confronts higher education: some are ready to face it contentedly not clearly knowing why, how, and in which ways we ought to change, whereas others, more reasonable and sensible, warn of dangers that lie ahead.

I shall not focus on describing the current problems of higher education, or even analyze the causes for such problems. Nor will I discuss the dangers that lie ahead of us, which cause paralysis and distortion of the issues. We must move on such a difficult ground cautiously.

According to the Bologna Agreement, all universities in Europe must adopt the new European standard for higher education, which is to be materialized in 2010. For some, this external requirement is a good opportunity of which we must take advantage. For others, and that includes me, it is a necessity. This European convergence will facilitate the exchange of students and teachers, assist in the recognition and professional profiling of degrees, and outline the best way to insert students into the job market. It will also require a deep transformation of the curriculum in its design, development, and assessment. The curriculum must show a correct balance between the contents of each area of knowledge and the competence that will be required in one's professional performance. A deep methodological change is also equally important, since the validity of the knowledge we must learn is strongly conditioned by how it is learned. Therefore, more autonomous and collaborative learning must be encouraged. For these reasons, a new role for both the students in the classroom and, of course, the teacher is demanded.

All of this leads us to reposition ourselves. The development of a new culture will be necessary, along with new ways of organizing and managing universities. More collaborative work will be needed. We should deepen and advance research in a fairer, more creative, and supportive way. It is also necessary to promote and support the improvement of university teaching, to recover a critical university innovative spirit, and to make the administrative, service, and technical staff participants in the project. We must listen and answer to the social demands and needs as quickly and adequately as possible. We must also contribute to changing and improving social structures by positioning ourselves near the weak and deprived, the minorities and the excluded. In this way we can create fairer and more supportive structures. We can also dignify the human condition by working to diminish violence and complexity within this supposedly developed society.

Understanding this, Lasallian universities must embark upon a very complex and uncertain journey, without doubt, but one that requires an adventurous spirit. We should be able to take risks, lead the way, free ourselves from unnecessary weight, and use our intuition in a rigorous and creative way so that we know what we shall need in order to face the unknown, what is emerging. Thus we will be able to answer with the spirit that has characterized us from the beginning: faith and zeal. Our Founder knew how to answer to the needs of his time and to advance from one commitment to another. We should be on the lookout for the new needs of both the young and adults of today, and we should commit ourselves to them in their training and the exercise of their profession. We should see that they keep improving themselves throughout their lives based not only on rigorous, updated, and valid knowledge, but also on the faith that inspires every human being. Faith is the focus of their lives; it liberates them and makes them stretch further from their own limits. It generates values and attitudes that will allow them to exercise their profession with a greater human quality, with kindness and harmony, with justice and fairness.

In view of this situation, I would like to provide some lines of action or challenges to be considered when facing the change and transformation of our universities.

1. Answering to a Need Shared by All the Members of the University Community

In determining our answer to a need shared by all the members of the community, we should start with a shared reflection on our own practice, examining what we have done previously and what our current situation is. In this way, we could analyze the baselines on which to project improvement, adapting our universities to improved internal and external requirements.

It is important to involve everybody. And when I say everybody, I mean directors, teachers, administration, services and technical staff, students, and collaborators. Far from distracting us, complicating the analysis, slowing down the processes, etc., this approach allows us to face issues in a more precise engagement, and it will guarantee our success.

Answering to external demands is not enough. It is also necessary that we discover together, from within the university, why change is important, what are our aims for designing and dealing with projects, and especially how we are going to favor it. The process, deadlines, and collaborations will be clearly delineated.

2. Generating or Increasing a Larger Culture of Collaboration Inside and Outside Universities

It is more and more necessary to deepen collaboration and thus realize a more collective work.

The most common culture in the educational context is that of individualism. In 1989, Rosenholts commented that in effective schools, "it is assumed that improvement in teaching is a collective issue rather than an individual one and that the analysis, evaluation, and experimentation, when carried out together with colleagues, are the conditions in which teachers learn and improve."

On the other hand, Hargreaves and Fullas point out that we should avoid two dangers in this school culture of collaboration: fragmentation (which takes place within a cycle or stage and not among cycles or among the different stages) and fake collectivity (which is on papers but not in life).

This way, there are two axes with multiple branches:

- *Internal collaboration* among all the members of the university community: teachers with students, teachers with teachers, teachers and administration and services staff, among departments, among degrees, etc. There are many ways, levels, modalities, and areas of collaboration in the different actions and projects that are developed in the classrooms, by faculties, and in the university.

  It will not be an easy target to hit. We come from an individualistic culture, marked by bad experiences and many failures when trying to deal with projects in universities in a joint way. If this were not enough, we lack the training and mastery of competences and, in some cases, the necessary basic abilities that are needed to establish collaborations and successful teamwork.

- *External collaboration.* Every university willing to provide a better service to its environment and to society must strengthen its offer with a universe of relations and collaborations outside its own campus and aside from its daily work.

  Establishing agreements with other universities, companies, institutions, public administrations, associations, and individuals is a common practice and one on the increase in recent years. Our universities have a great number of agreements that favor the mobility of students and teachers and allow the development of research programs while providing and sharing resources.

3. The Creation of Knowledge Networks for Transferring and Creating New "Products," Especially Among Lasallian Universities

One of our most urgent present challenges is being able to create networks that will allow a close collaboration among Lasallian universities. The collective exchange of beneficial programs and successful actions, as well as the opportunity to create together, would strengthen all of our universities. It would also allow us to better fulfill our institutional objectives. In this way we could provide better service to our local social settings as well as to the internal environment of our Lasallian institution.

For that, we must advance in what is known today as knowledge management. Though there are not as yet clear models for knowledge management or knowledge creation, it should not dissuade us or slow us down from developing these fields. It should rather encourage us to enter this field by creating and sharing our knowledge of management and development of knowledge networks with others.

As Joaquín Gairín (2005) highlights in his article "Knowledge Management Network," Nonaka and Takeuchi (1999) present their organizational knowledge creation theory, which results in a model for knowledge management focused on the mobilization and conversion of tacit knowledge (epistemological dimension) and the creation of organizational knowledge into individual knowledge (ontological dimension).

According to the authors, organizational knowledge creation is a spiral process that is produced by the interaction between the epistemological and ontological dimensions through time that will constitute the third and final dimension.

This interaction between different types and levels of knowledge is carried out by the people who are a key factor in this model. The "spiral of knowledge" is set in motion by means of group-dialogue sessions, where people reveal and share their tacit knowledge with the rest of the group through metaphors and analogies. This model of knowledge creation and management is represented in a cyclical and never-ending model consisting of five stages.

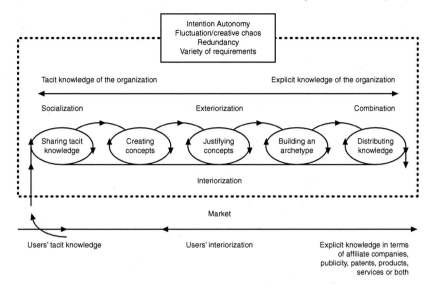

Five-stage model for the management knowledge creation process (Nonaka and Takeuchi, 1999)

The creation of these networks is not an easy task. They are a combination of three factors that require our attention in order to obtain a high performance in the operating capacity of these knowledge networks. These three factors are knowledge management, cooperative work, and technologies.

It will be necessary to create and participate in voluntary virtual communities made of representative members of each Lasallian university. There must be institutional support and enough autonomy and independence. In these virtual communities, the relation and cooperation must be reinforced so that the coldness and lack of physical presence of the virtual factor is overcome. Other aspects that will need reinforcement are working group cohesion in the search for that explicit common knowledge, developing communicative skills, and overcoming the mere exchange of information to be able to generate new knowledge. To do so, it is important to have not only a good moderator on the network but also a good knowledge manager. The former must accompany and facilitate the dialogue process in the virtual community. S/he will favor the improvement and enrichment of the participations and will also favor conflict resolution, autonomous work, etc. In conclusion, the aim is not only to achieve the transference of each institution's knowledge but also to be able to produce new knowledge.

4. Improving, Dignifying, and Crediting University Teaching

Every university has three important purposes: teaching, research, and providing a service to society. However, having said that, teaching is often the least emphasized of the three. More importance is given to research, innovation, and the development of new, more useful, and effective products for society. When Fairweah (1993) studied the connection between teaching and the salaries of 8,383 teachers in 424 universities in the USA, he concluded the following: "Teachers who devote more time to research and publication and less time to teaching are better paid."

We must promote a real improvement in teaching at our universities. For that, we must support the teachers with training programs and encourage the implementation of best practices. This methodological commitment in the universities is not merely an individual commitment; it is also a collective one. If we teach together, we must train together for a better performance. We must also agree on the goals to be achieved and the teaching/methodological processes to be followed.

Furthermore, this dimension is fully connected to our tradition. We have always been characterized by teaching and by being very aware of the teaching-learning process.

5. Facilitating Access to All So That No Individual Is Excluded

Achieving this goal is not easy, mainly because of compelling economic factors. However, we have to continue developing large doses of creativity in order to find financing and adequate grants so that everybody is cared for. The increasing commitment of our universities to reach the underprivileged is very encouraging. A good example of this is the creation of Universidad La Salle Netzahualcóyotl, supported by ULSA, in Mexico City.

Favoring and facilitating the access to those who are discriminated against on the grounds of their creed, race, and culture is then another goal.

Lasallian centers always have been and must continue to be platforms for dialogue between creeds and cultures. This enriching and productive dialogue is especially important in today's climate of societal division, fragmentation, and confrontation, sometimes due to fundamentalism and "purity of race."

We must welcome those who have a slower learning pace or who have some disability by removing barriers. We ought to reduce the physical, teaching, and organizational barriers to facilitate everyone's access. This means training the teachers, having specialized teachers, and having adapted resources so that we can respond to multiple disabilities and diverse needs.

6. IT Supporting University Management and Teaching: A Tool to Facilitate Everybody's Access

In the face of the change and transformation of our universities, we must carry out a detailed analysis on the advantages of technology in the teaching-learning process, whether it is traditional or online learning.

Informational technology (IT) favors communication, the exchange of information, synchronous and asynchronous participation, as well as individual, autonomous, and collaborative work. New tools appear every day, and there are others that can be designed and adapted to communicative and teaching needs in order to improve communication, teaching, learning, and the construction of knowledge.

The great challenge in this area is not in having more and better technological devices and tools, but rather in the use we make of them and how we incorporate them to the training and research process at universities. For this reason, the training of teachers and the university community in general is essential. It is also necessary to create a new culture so that we can communicate via e-mail and engage digital platforms. We can then meet, dialogue, and collaborate in a virtual way. It is a challenging road with dangers: we will have to work on group cohesion, communication blockages, participation motivations, and verbal exchanges in much the same way as we do in situations where we are physically present.

These tools neither substitute for nor compete against the value of traditional learning. I believe that we are all committing ourselves not to distance learning but to blended learning. Physical presence in communication and training processes for virtual discussions are essential (the details of which are not appropriate for this essay). Physical presence can be considered on many different levels.

According to what I have said in the previous paragraph, it is more and more necessary to have virtual platforms at universities to make blended learning possible. Increasingly, students work or perform multiple activities at the same time. Additionally, we need to provide our students with both in-service and lifelong training at Lasallian centers of higher education.

Moreover, according to challenge number 3, we must take significant steps to learn about the different digital platforms we are using in each Lasallian university. We must also approximate them and even come to a certain homogenization in our aim to face the challenges of the creation of knowledge networks, joint training, and research programs.

In order for this to be successful, the same teaching model should be used as a framework for training programs that are to be designed and developed together.

7. Social Commitment and Community Development: A Growing Reality in Our Universities

Following the most genuine tradition in our Institute, and with the support of our documents and the recommendations of our Brother Superior General, Lasallian universities have been adding a significant number of teaching hours to the curriculum. We have also added intervention hours in the social and natural setting whether immediate or far away. The objective is for the students to receive practical training and, at the same time, obtain an intimate knowledge of the social reality in which we live. Then they can discover any existing inequalities or injustices and commit themselves to actions that address these issues.

We should share programs and best practices, develop voluntary work projects, and require training. We should also try to encourage philanthropic service and volunteerism as personal lifelong commitments and professional activities.

8. The Creation of an Innovation Park and an Intervention Center

Several Lasallian universities already have an Innovation Park and/or an Intervention Center on their campus.

No doubt, such initiatives foster innovation, research, and close collaboration with the social setting. For this reason, as well as for many others, universities should not withdraw into themselves but rather remain open to the outside by establishing a productive dialogue: listening and being aware of external needs. In this way demands can be answered promptly, with flexibility and certainty. The answer must never be linear but critical, going further from what is merely expected toward making a genuinely transformative improvement.

The Intervention Centers (Center for Clinic Psychology, Day Care Centers, Rehabilitation Centers, Early Attention Centers, consultancy firms, and Assessment Centers) give both teachers and students the possibility of direct contact with the outside, the possibility to professionally develop their practice, and the opportunity to conduct research, test programs, and develop new knowledge. At the same time, these centers provide social services of great quality.

Serving as a company incubator, Innovation Parks are a door to innovation. They establish the right conditions to create potentially successful initiatives.

Many of the parks are related to the fields of management and technology. We must also promote Innovation Parks in the fields of social services, education, and international cooperation. Our facilities must foster innovation.

Our universities have to join efforts by sharing the array of agreements and collaborations we already have developed. These parks enable our university projects to be more meaningful and successful.

Conclusion

I am aware that there are many remaining challenges. I also know that I have not mentioned many of the projects we are carrying out that are closely related to our tradition and to the most genuine aspect of De La Salle. I wanted to share what was most urgent and new from my point of view. However, I did not want at all to undervalue or discredit the many good actions that already have been achieved.

We have the necessary strength. While there will be challenges to confront, we will be successful if we work creatively and collaboratively in responding to them.

Author Biography

Br. Juan Antonio Ojeda is dean of the La Salle Center for University Studies. Additionally, he is president of the Association of University Teaching Centers for the Church on a national level. A professor of instruction and teaching organization, Brother Juan Antonio serves on the permanent commission of the National Conference of Deans and Directors of Education and Teaching.

CAN A UNIVERSITY WITH A MULTIFAITH EDUCATIONAL COMMUNITY BE CATHOLIC AND LASALLIAN?

By: Br. John Johnston, FSC

The organizers of *Reflections on Lasallian Higher Education* have invited several of us to share perspectives on Lasallian higher education, granting us the liberty to draw upon our personal experience and viewpoints and to take an approach we consider appropriate.

Over the years I have had occasion to speak on the historical context of Lasallian higher education and to reflect on characteristics that Lasallian institutions must manifest. My approach in this essay is different. I reflect upon the lived experience of a specific institution that defines itself as *Catholic and Lasallian with a multifaith educational community*. I consider its quest for self-understanding and identity. The institution is Christian Brothers University (CBU), Memphis, Tennessee, USA. CBU was known as Christian Brothers College (CBC) for much of its 135-year history.

The origin of this essay is an address I delivered to the CBU faculty and staff in August 2005. My approach is not scholarly. It is one of gathering pertinent information, commenting on issues and questions, and proposing challenges the institution needs to consider. I write as a catalyst, not an expert. My purpose is limited: to focus on the *Catholic* dimension of Christian Brothers University and to place on the table information and thoughts that will promote reflection and dialogue. I hope that this essay might contribute to the ongoing conversation about being Catholic and Lasallian in the increasingly pluralistic situations in which we offer Lasallian higher education. I hope also that this conversation might lead to constructive decisions.

History of CBU: 1871–2006

Christian Brothers College came into existence in 1871. It functioned as a combined elementary school, high school, and college. It granted high school diplomas, as well as bachelor's and master's degrees until 1915. The exodus of students for military service during World War I led to suspension of the college division. CBC dropped elementary classes in 1922. From that time until 1940, the institution operated as a high school only. The college division reopened in 1940, first as a junior college, then, in 1953, as a four-year college. The high school division separated in 1965, moving to a new location. Christian Brothers College became coeducational in 1970 and reintroduced graduate-level programs and degrees in 1987. Three years later, in 1990, Christian Brothers College became Christian Brothers University. Today there are some 1,900 students.

Catholic and Interfaith

In its mission statement, CBU describes itself as a Catholic institution of higher education in the tradition of the Christian Brothers. A significant number of CBU students are from greater Memphis and surrounding areas, where the Catholic population is small. The Diocese of Memphis reports a Catholic population of 4.5%. The percentage in the Memphis metropolitan area is slightly higher. Published statistics indicate that students at CBU are of more than thirty religious traditions:

Catholic	22%
Other Christian	42%
Muslim	0.3%
Jewish	0.2%
Other faith	2%
Not declared	33%

The questionnaire that provided the above information grants the students the freedom to respond or not to respond. For perhaps a variety of reasons, one-third do not declare a religious faith or denomination.

The CBU Web site says that while CBU is a Catholic university, religious beliefs and affiliation are very diverse. Religious observances are not required, but students are encouraged to practice their faith openly and actively. The office of campus ministry supports a variety of programs that encourage students to explore their religious beliefs.

Nowhere is there an attempt to explain or even describe the *Catholic* nature of CBU or to respond to an obvious question: what is the relationship between *Catholic and interfaith?* CBU declares itself on the one hand to be a *Catholic* institution and on the other hand to be an *interfaith* educational community. Are these two claims compatible? How does this community, given its ecumenical and interreligious nature, relate to *Catholic?* Would it be more appropriate for Christian Brothers University to declare itself a nondenominational, ecumenical, interfaith, or even secular institution? It is useful to consider this question in a historic context. What has been and what is the experience of Lasallian mission over the years in Memphis and throughout the world?

Interfaith Lasallian Educational Communities in Memphis

From its earliest days, Christian Brothers College welcomed elementary, secondary, and tertiary level young people of all religious faiths. Long before substantial talk and action about "ecumenism" and "interfaith" dialogue, the Brothers and their collaborators respected the religious beliefs of students, parents, faculty, and staff that were not Catholic. This spirit continues today in the four Memphis Lasallian institutions: university, high school, and two elementary schools. In a remarkable statement in 1948, Mayor Watkins Overton described Christian Brothers College as a "temple of tolerance":

> Probably the greatest contribution that Christian Brothers College has made to the welfare of the city of Memphis was best expressed by his Eminence, Cardinal Stritch, a former resident of this city, when he said:

> *Christian Brothers College is a **Temple of Tolerance**, and has done more than any one factor I know of to break down religious prejudice in Memphis.* Through the halls of CBC have walked several generations of Catholics, Jews, and Protestants. By the thousands these alumni of Christian Brothers College of various faiths have lived in their lives an eloquent testimony to the ideals and principles, the understanding, and tolerance which they imbibed as students of the Brothers.

Interfaith Educational Communities Worldwide

Lasallian mission is a reality today in eighty countries. Nearly 80,000 Lasallian educators are at the service of some 900,000 students in more than one thousand institutions at all levels of education. Some sixty-five of these institutions are higher educational institutions. Many have large student populations. According to the International Association of Lasallian Universities, approximately half of the 900,000 Lasallian students are in higher education.

Although precise statistics are not available, Lasallian students, of whatever age, are Catholic, Orthodox, Protestant, Jewish, Muslim, Buddhist, Hindu, Confucianist, Shintoist, followers of traditional religions . . . or do not acknowledge any religious faith. An overwhelming majority of students in the Middle East, Turkey, and Pakistan are Muslim. The majority in India are Hindu. In Thailand, over 95% of our students are Buddhists. Members of Lasallian educational communities in Malaysia are Muslim, Buddhist, Hindu, and Christian. The harmony that normally reigns among students, faculty, and staff is striking. Striking also is the loyalty that is evident among former students who are not Christian and the pride they express in the education they have received.

Experience of John Baptist de La Salle

John Baptist de La Salle called the schools he founded *Christian* schools, and the society of Brothers he founded to run the schools Brothers of the *Christian* Schools. Because he used the word *Christian*, one might be tempted to credit De La Salle with pioneering in the ecumenical movement. Such a reading, however, would be false. For De La Salle and for his French compatriots in general, to be Christian was to be Catholic; to be Catholic was to be Christian. For De La Salle those who claimed to be Christian but not Catholic were heretics.

Nevertheless, it is interesting to recall a development that reveals, in the judgment of historian Henri Bédel, FSC, an attitude and sensitivity among De La Salle and the early Brothers that, to an extent at least, points to the commitment of their successors to educate children, youth, and adults, and to work with teachers of non-Catholic religions.

In 1685, Louis XIV, King of France, abrogated the Edict of Nantes, which had granted Protestants freedom of conscience, political rights, and limited freedom of worship. Many Protestants fled abroad. Some adopted the Catholic faith more or less willingly and were known as the "new converts." Their children had to be baptized and educated in the Catholic faith. Many new converts, however, remained attached to Protestantism. Others, referred to as Camisards, because of the white shirt that distinguished them, resisted by force. These Protestants were Calvinists. Catholics called them Huguenots, a name they considered offensive.

De La Salle accepted an invitation to begin a school that would be open to children of new converts. Later the Brothers accepted a second school. The challenge was to win the hearts of the children and to overcome the prejudices of their parents. Bédel says that the Brothers succeeded:

> When they taught Catholic doctrine, they did so without polemics. When the book they used spoke of heretics, it did so in general terms and never used the words "Protestants," "Calvinists," or "Huguenots." … The Brothers gave a picture of Catholicism different from the one prevalent among Protestants. The attitude of the Brothers regarding a particular area of religious sensitivity contained in embryonic form the ability of their successors to educate children and to work with teachers from non-Catholic religions. (*The Origins: 1651–1726*)

Lasallian Mission: Promoting the Reign of God Through Education

Stated succinctly, to be Christian is to be a follower of Jesus. It is to be caught up in and transformed by his story, his teaching, his passage from death to life, his saving grace. To be Christian is to share Jesus' mission of proclaiming and promoting the kingdom of God. When Jesus proclaims the kingdom, he proclaims God's unconditional love, a love that challenges and calls for wholehearted acceptance, a love that demands love of neighbor. To accept God's love is be transformed by it, to become persons totally committed to others in love.

John Paul II says the kingdom is a call to universal brotherhood and sisterhood because all are sons and daughters of the same God and all have the right to live with dignity, in justice, and in peace. The Church, he says, is to be the sign and instrument of the kingdom, proclaiming and promoting it as Jesus did.

Lasallians constitute an international association of persons sharing in the mission of the Catholic Church. The Lasallian mission is to promote the kingdom of God through education. Lasallians engaged in higher education are uniquely situated to help young people liberate themselves from all that holds them back from being the persons God wants them to be, to help them develop their God-given talents, to help them become persons—whatever their religious faith—committed to building a world where people can live as sons and daughters of God and as brothers and sisters.

That said, we have to return to the question we asked before: our past and present commitment to young people of all religious faiths notwithstanding, are we really justified in calling schools *Catholic* when the community of students, teachers, and staff are of a variety of faiths? Does it make sense to call Christian Brothers University a Catholic institution when only a fourth of the students are Catholic? Would it be more appropriate or even more honest to declare CBU nondenominational, ecumenical, interfaith, or even secular?

My answer is an emphatic *no*. I shall attempt to explain this response.

Some Pertinent Thoughts

My purpose in this essay is to provide information and thoughts that will contribute to the ongoing conversation about being Catholic, not only at Christian Brothers University, but also at other institutions of higher education in religiously pluralistic situations.

It is helpful, I think, to reflect on the religious dimension of CBU in light of the following pertinent thoughts:

1. John Paul II

> The Church, precisely because it is Catholic, is open to dialogue with all other Christians, with the followers of non-Christian religions, and with all people of good will.

The Pope does not say that "in spite of" being Catholic, the Church is open to dialogue, but "precisely because" it is Catholic. This remarkable statement witnesses to a stance in the Catholic Church that is of major importance today. When the Church uses the word *dialogue*, it means relationships on a number of levels: fraternal relations, collaboration in providing social services, collaboration in the quest for justice and peace, prayer together in appropriate ways, informal conversations about religious beliefs, and formal theological considerations of religious beliefs.

Catholic universities and colleges need to be centers of dialogue. Levels attained will vary. Students, faculty, and staff at Christian Brothers University grow in fraternal relations, provide service to the needy, collaborate in various ways in promotion of peace and justice, pray together on occasion. I have no doubt that at least some of them converse about personal religious beliefs. Since all students take courses in religious studies, there is a degree at least of theological discussion of differences.

To promote dialogue on these various levels is to live the *Catholic* dimension of CBU.

2. Michael Miller

In June 2005, Canadian Archbishop Michael Miller, secretary of the Vatican Congregation for Catholic Education, wrote in *America* magazine:

> Some academics, albeit probably a minority, are uncomfortable with the coupling of "Catholic identity" and "interreligious dialogue." . . . For them, such an undertaking would be a sign of weakness or even a betrayal of faith.

> Despite this view, a good argument can be made to show that a university's Catholic identity is in fact strengthened when it fosters interreligious dialogue by introducing students to knowledge of other religions and by encouraging research in this field. . . . There is no reason to fear that interreligious dialogue in any way compromises an institution's Catholic identity. Precisely as Catholic, a university should recognize that the way of dialogue is the way of the Church.

Archbishop Miller's focus is on dialogue among Christians and non-Christians. Nevertheless, his words are applicable also to ecumenical dialogue, that is to say, dialogue among Christians.

3. John Jenkins

In his inaugural address, Holy Cross Father John Jenkins, new president of Notre Dame, made these pertinent remarks:

> We must recognize and affirm the value of religious diversity at Notre Dame. Within our community are Protestant and Orthodox Christians, Jews, Muslims, Hindus, Buddhists, and those of other religious traditions and no religious tradition. As we affirm our Catholic identity, we acknowledge and embrace the many non-Catholics who are deeply committed to this university and its principles. If we were exclusively Catholic, we would be less

catholic—less broad, less universal, with fewer opportunities to enrich our dialogue and test our ideas with those who share many of our values but not all our views.

While I believe Father Jenkins' words are pertinent, I readily acknowledge that the percentage of Catholics among students at Notre Dame is more than three times that of CBU.

4. *The Ecumenical Directory*, Vatican, 1993

This document contains statements that many find surprising. I have paraphrased these statements from sections 68, 85, and 141:

> Schools of every kind and grade should give an ecumenical dimension to religious teaching and should educate for dialogue, peace, and personal relationships. Teachers, therefore, must have correct and adequate information about churches and ecclesial communities, especially those that exist in their region.

> Catholic schools and institutions should make every effort to respect the faith and conscience of students or teachers who belong to other Churches or ecclesial communities. Authorities should take care that clergy of other communities have every facility for giving spiritual and sacramental ministration to their own faithful who attend such schools or institutions. When circumstances allow, authorities can offer them their facilities, including the church or chapel.

5. The Diocese of Memphis

Since the Jubilee Year of 2000, the diocese has reopened seven inner-city Catholic primary schools, two of which are in the Lasallian network. Another will open in September 2006. In the same month a diocesan Catholic high school will adopt the corporate internship model. Extraordinary contributions have made this incredible accomplishment possible. While donors remain anonymous, it is known that many are not Catholic. Moreover, the overwhelming majority of students in these schools are not Catholic. Not a few people have wondered about this remarkable commitment of the Church to the education of youth who are not Catholic. Bishop Terry Steib, SVD, and Dr. Mary McDonald, Superintendent of Catholic Schools, respond:

> We teach, not because the students are Catholic, but because WE are Catholic.

A Distinct Understanding of "Religious" University

I believe the thoughts just expressed can help explain how CBU can call itself "Catholic in the Lasallian tradition." At the same time, we need to recognize that this understanding of being "religious" differs, sometimes significantly, from the understanding of some other "religious" colleges and universities.

After visiting and studying twenty religiously affiliated higher education institutions, Naomi Schaefer Riley, reporter for the *Wall Street Journal*, wrote *God on the Quad: How Religious Colleges and the Missionary Generation Are Changing America*, published in 2005. The study includes institutions that are Mormon, Catholic, Evangelical, Baptist, Jewish, and Buddhist. Many of the institutions visited, including some of the Catholic schools, resemble in various degrees "seminaries" or "houses of formation." They require public expressions of belief and fidelity to specific religious observances. Regulations governing student life are strict. Some of the universities expect their students to evangelize, often meaning "to proselytize," before and after graduation.

Christian Brothers University defines itself as a "religious" university, but its understanding of *religious* differs from that of most of the schools in Riley's study. Consequently, it is essential that CBU articulate precisely what being "Catholic in the Lasallian tradition" means. Obviously, it means offering theology and/or religious studies courses that are intellectually substantial, challenging, and stimulating; maintaining a vibrant campus ministry program that administration and faculty strongly support; and displaying religious signs and symbols that remind all that the institution is Catholic.

Still, being "Catholic in the Lasallian tradition" means more. Catholic identity must be *evident* in all aspects of university life: strategic planning, curriculum, faculty policies, student life policies, finances, etc. It must be manifest in a strong spirit of community on campus. Students, administrators, faculty, and staff must, to the extent possible, know one another and manifest mutual respect and active concern. Catholic identity in the Lasallian tradition will be a reality only if members of the educational community interiorize that identity and commit themselves to living it. John Paul II writes that Catholic institutions promote dialogue *because* they are Catholic. Michael Miller says that it is *precisely* as Catholic that the university enters into dialogue. Consistent with this line of thought, it is because we are a Catholic institution that we are committed to fraternal relations with people of diverse faiths. This commitment to dialogue makes intelligible a Catholic university with a multifaith educational community.

The CBU educational community of students, board, administrators, faculty, and staff must be a community of persons who, regardless of personal beliefs, understand, recognize, foster, and defend the Catholic identity of the institution. They must be persons committed to unity in diversity. This commitment is far from reducing religious beliefs to the lowest common denominator for the sake of uniformity. It is far also from promoting unity through "neutrality" or through "privatization" of religious beliefs. On the contrary, CBU must be a community in which everybody enjoys genuine religious freedom, a freedom that totally excludes any expectation that members of the educational community have to "privatize" or "bracket" their beliefs. All must be free to express their beliefs and know that others will respect them.

I stated above that the religious dimension includes but is not limited to solid academic courses or to strong campus ministry program:

> Teachers exercise a religious mission whenever they truly educate. They exercise a mission when they awaken in students a serious attitude toward life, lead them to experience the autonomy of personal thought, help them overcome their personal prejudices and peer pressure, teach them how to listen and to try to understand, to be open to others, to trust, and to love. (*A Declaration: The Brother in the Modern World*, 1967)

CBU is currently engaged in several initiatives to strengthen Catholic and Lasallian identity: the strategic planning process, new academic programs, reform of general education requirements to make more aspects of classical liberal education available to all, greater emphasis on ethical leadership, and development of a new interdisciplinary core curriculum. Dr. Anthony Aretz, academic vice-president, writes, "The core curriculum, philosophy, religion, service learning, and the entire CBU educational experience can create an interfaith educational experience that educates our students towards the highest ideals of both private and public virtue."

Our Students

No discussion about Christian Brothers University as a Catholic university would be complete without some reflections on the students for whom the institution exists. I mentioned earlier that two-thirds of the student body declare affiliation with some religion or Church, while one-third do not. In my opinion, it is difficult if not impossible to draw meaningful conclusions from the responses of either group. It is useful, however, to take into serious consideration two recent studies.

The first is the *National Study of Youth*, conducted in 2002–2003 by researchers at the University of North Carolina. They surveyed 3,370 teenagers—not yet but future college students—816 of whom were Catholic. Two of the researchers report and analyze the complex but fascinating findings in the very readable *Soul Searching: The Religious and Spiritual Lives of American Teenagers.*

The University of California at Los Angeles (UCLA) conducted the second study. Researchers surveyed 112,232 freshmen in 236 randomly selected United States institutions. Organizers have published findings at *www.spirituality.ucla.edu.* To the surprise of many, the surveys reveal a high level of interest and involvement in spirituality and religion. Moreover, these freshmen express high expectations of the role universities ought to play in their spiritual and emotional development:

- 80% are interested in spirituality.

- 76% are searching for meaning or purpose in life.

- 74% discuss the meaning of life with friends.

- 81% attend religious services.

- 80% discuss religion and spirituality with friends.

- 79% believe in God.

- 69% pray.

- 68% expect their college or university to help them with self-understanding and in developing personal values.

- 48% want the institution to encourage their personal expression of spirituality.

- 8% say their professors encourage discussion of religious or spiritual matters or provide opportunities to discuss the purpose and meaning of life.

Implications

What are some implications of these reflections for CBU board members, administrators, faculty, staff, and students?

CBU board, administrators, faculty, and staff:

- must be *intentional* and *proactive* in articulating the identity of CBU as Catholic and Lasallian and must commit themselves to making CBU be the institution it purports to be. The consequences of a *passive, pro forma* stance are inevitable: the Catholic identity of Christian Brothers University will erode—not by decision, but by default—the experience of not-a-few once religiously affiliated colleges and universities in the United States

- must be ready to address the questions and concerns of students who are searching for meaning, youth with profound religious, philosophical, and moral questions

- must be disposed to "walk with" students, to take them seriously, to share with them their vision, beliefs, and hopes, always allowing students the freedom to express their questions and to seek their answers

Students must have opportunities:

- to pursue truth and knowledge in a faith-inspired atmosphere free from any kind of political correctness, whether of the right or of the left

- to grow in religious and philosophical knowledge through excellent courses and seminars taught by highly qualified professors

- to pursue truth outside their specialties

- to live their faith with others of faith

- if Catholic, to participate in well-prepared and appropriate Eucharistic celebrations, especially on Sunday

- if not Catholic, to participate in appropriate religious services, on campus if there is the demand

- to participate in periodic prayer services for all

In Conclusion ...

Permit me to share some personal convictions:

- Christian Brothers University is justified in calling itself a Catholic university in the Lasallian tradition with a multifaith educational community.

- Board members, administrators, faculty, and staff must be able to articulate in a straightforward, unambiguous fashion how CBU understands itself as Catholic and Lasallian.

- Authentic living of its Catholic and Lasallian identity is intimately related to the vitality of Christian Brothers University.

- The vitality of CBU is intimately related to success in recruitment and in institutional advancement.

- The future, therefore, of Christian Brothers University is contingent upon clarity of identity and passionate commitment to living this identity.

- CBU has a religious heritage of which all can be justifiably proud.

- CBU has a heritage to acknowledge, articulate, and foster.

- CBU has a heritage to build upon for the future.

Author Biography

Br. John Johnston was for many years Vicar General, then Superior General of the De La Salle Christian Brothers. He served as assistant special secretary for the Synod on Consecrated Life and was vice president of the Union of Superiors General in Rome. More recently, he has served as the USA/Toronto Regional Director of Education and as a senior consultant for the Lasallian Association for Mission.

REINTERPRETING DE LA SALLE

By: Carmelita I. Quebengco

The Lasallian mission is to provide a human and Christian education to the young, especially the poor. Understanding its many implications and applications to current realities would require a review of its foundation and development, dating back to the seventeenth century. As Botana (2004, p. 22) wrote: "At that time John Baptist was just twenty-eight years old. Adrien Nyel had come to Rheims, John Baptist's hometown, with the idea of founding a school for poor children." John Baptist was convinced that the project was worthwhile and offered to help.

De La Salle was moved by the situation of the students, children of artisans and the poor, who were abandoned and left to themselves. He soon realized too that although Nyel was a compassionate man and an idealist, he was not a hands-on school administrator. Among the existing school problems, De La Salle saw teacher incompetence as needing the most attention. The teachers were ill prepared for the tasks, needed guidance, and knew very little about pedagogy. This condition made him think very seriously about how to improve the quality of education being implemented; thus began the Lasallian mission and conduct of schools. Botana (2004, p. 60) continues, "From that point on, we see the development of an inter relation of persons, needs, aims and structures." As De La Salle focused his attention and exerted all efforts in helping develop teachers and improve the administration of the school, he himself was transformed.

On June 6, 1694, De La Salle and twelve associates came together as a community and solemnly promised to commit themselves for life to the Lasallian mission. The following passage from Rummery (2004) serves as the foundational pattern of the Lasallian shared mission and association:

What bound members of the community together were not the traditional bonds of a religious community, but the willingness of a group of laymen to associate themselves, in order to assure the continuity of the gratuitous school. . . . Commitment was expressed through the willingness and availability of members to continue the work that had been begun. If De La Salle allowed some to take vows, it was to accommodate their own preference and devotion. The common mission would be served by all, with or without vows. (p. 4)

Throughout his life, De La Salle introduced several innovations, among which are the following: the system of simultaneous instruction and the use of the vernacular as medium of instruction, establishment of sixty schools all over France including the first normal school to be founded in 1685, writing of twenty articles and handbooks on education and the management of schools. These accomplishments earned for him the privilege of being listed as one of the "pioneers of modern education." It is no surprise at all that he is the Patron of Teachers. When leaders tended to be autocratic, De La Salle was no authoritarian, perhaps because he believed too much in the equality of persons and their empowerment. For example, Botana (2004, p. 23) describes De La Salle's style in solving school problems in this manner: "The observations of De La Salle and each Brother were exchanged and improved upon community sessions. . . . They shared their ideas, discerned what was going on, and managed to create a style, a way of acting, a kind of school . . ."

Michel Sauvage in Rummery (2004, p. 3) notes in *Catechese et Laicat* the insistence of De La Salle that "the journey of faith was not to be made alone but was to be sustained through membership of a community." This concept is now part of the Lasallian tradition and the foundational model of a Lasallian school community. Hence, the journey toward the fulfillment of mission is not the responsibility only of administrators, nor of those who have served the school longer, but together and by association, of all educators in a school community.

Fundamental Concepts in the Schools of De La Salle

To De La Salle, the realization of the glory of God, which has been defined by St. Irenaeus of Lyons (Botana, 2004, p. 47) as "the human person fully alive" is the reason for a school's being. His compassion and sensitivity to the needs of society, which then as now call for transformation, led him to prioritize the education of children from poor families and turned it into his lifetime commitment. These young people are to be embraced as they are, where they are and a school is to "save them by means of an education that touches not only their minds but also their hearts . . . that saves them for freedom and dignity and their rightful place in the world" (Meister, 2004, p. 4). In this concept, education liberates and develops students to become men and women fully alive. Pedro Gil (2004, p. 1) adds that the challenge of mission is not in the technical or material order. It is something much more remote. It does not refer to our work but to its meaning. This meaning is broadened to include effort in transforming society as captured by Van Grieken (1999) in his description of De La Salle as an educational leader:

> De La Salle stands out as someone who held the demands of faith higher than the demands of society. Where society insisted on close distinctions, De La Salle broke those distinctions by his admission policies and seating arrangement. Where society established strong educational limitations based on status, privilege, and connections, De La Salle kept his teachers focused on the needs of students. Where society provided education for the poor in order to keep them under control and prepare to enter society's work force, De La Salle provided education as a means of liberating the poor, providing them some measure of control over their own future in society. Where society saw things through its own lens, De La Salle had only the open eyes of faith. (p. 131)

The main focus and priority in the schools of De La Salle were the students and their development. That was the reason and basis for everything done in school. Teachers considered themselves not only as mentors and facilitators for the students' acquisition of new knowledge and skills, but more important than those, as elder brothers and sisters, "guardian angels," and ministers of God's love, where there was always a special place for genuine concern and care for their students. Botana (2004, p. 33) quotes from De La Salle's *Meditation* to describe this: "He (God) looks upon them with compassion and watches over them as protector, support, and Father; but He does so by commissioning you (teachers) with this task." From this comes the spirituality of a Lasallian teacher, which is student oriented. To teach in a Lasallian school should be viewed not just as a means of livelihood, a profession, but above all a vocation, where teachers serve as a "sign of faith" to their students. This is symbolized by a star that usually appears in the logo of a Lasallian school. Not only faith but also zeal comprise the spirit of a Lasallian school. The zeal is self-effacement and commitment, exemplified by a teacher's dedication to the fulfillment of mission and genuine enthusiasm for this work. "The teacher lives for those that are entrusted to him/(her). He/(she) strives to promote their growth and so is always alert to initiatives in pedagogy that will renew the school and make it ever more effective" (Botana, 2004, p. 40). Through this, students are enabled to develop their full potentials and awaken themselves to the many possibilities for growth in and of society, rendering their teachers also as bringers of hope. Teaching becomes a vocation and is elevated at a level higher than work, profession, and the self. For the teachers, this experience can be so meaningful; it is transformative, resulting in a sharper, stronger sense of identity, a new way of being and relating among peers.

In the Lasallian paradigm, what gives life to a school is the community of persons committed to the same mission and who together seek and help each other to find the best means toward its fulfillment. This implies communion, a bond among members, borne out of open mindedness, communication at a deeper level, and sharing one's person. These acts energize community members, giving them a strong sense of solidarity. "The community is the teacher of teachers: it facilitates the formation of teachers, encourages the exchange of pedagogical experiences, and speeds up the search for the most effective methods. It assists in the acquisition of those values, which will then be passed on to the students. It promotes reflection on the reality of youth and their corresponding educational demands" (Botana, 2004, p. 14).

The schools founded by De La Salle were elementary schools, normal training academies, practical education programs for livelihood, and reformatory schools. His approach to school administration was from a very practical perspective. His vision and resulting educational programs were based on a combination of faith and immediate response to the needs of society and the poor. His administrative policies, priorities, and procedures were formulated to support these, as well as the development of a school community infused with faith and zeal. In developing and refining such policies and procedures, he relied on his, the Brothers', and the teachers' experience in the actual conduct of school.

Lasallian Education and Current Realities

More than three hundred years after its inception, the Lasallian mission to provide a human and Christian education to the young, especially the poor, remains relevant. Education continues to be cited as one of the basic and potent means to national development. Despite advancements in science and technology, higher levels of efficiency and productivity, instant communication with anyone anywhere in the world, and globalization, the poor fail to have equal access to needed basic resources and opportunities. Although globalization has its advantages, there are also unintended and unwanted consequences like consumerism, protectionism, and greed, the last believed to be widening the gap between the better off and the marginalized. Also, "the poor are victims of an educational and cultural model conceived usually for the exploitation of the world and its people" (Gil, 2004, p. 1).

The Lasallian mission originally referred to the economically poor and, in Lasallian schools, they continue to be the community's priority;

however, there is also more sensitivity now to other forms of poverty in the moral, affective, intellectual, and physical aspects. In the Philippine district, there are also schools that cater largely to students from the middle and upper socioeconomic classes. With this development comes the need to broaden perspectives to include other forms of poverty and to establish a clear relationship between school programs and the needs of a different society as part of mission. Particularly in the high tuition schools from where future leaders are expected to come, the offering of education programs for change that is pro poor, strong advocacy for social justice and a more human and just social order are in keeping with the Lasallian mission. This also serves to offer the students a very real, meaningful challenge as well as a clear sign of hope.

Following this lead, programs in a Lasallian school will have to be both present and future oriented, devoted to the holistic formation of students so they become active searchers and lovers of truth, with the appropriate attitudes and values, confident and courageous, and with a creative hope that will enable them to help transform society, rather than just passively joining it. Botana (2004, p. 95) specifies this further: "The best school is not the one that gives the most answers, but one that raises questions in a person's inner self, and encourages him/(her) to search for the answers."

In this set up, Declaration 41, as quoted by Botana (2004), states that Lasallian teachers are expected to

> awaken the young to an awareness that life is to be taken seriously and to the conviction of the greatness of human destiny; help them experience intellectual rigor and a desire to seek the truth, the autonomy of personal thought; help them use liberty to overcome their ready made prejudices and ideas, as well as overcome social pressures and those that derive from the forces of disintegration within the human person; dispose them to use their freedom, intelligence and training in the service of their fellow human beings; open them to others by teaching them how to listen and understand others; instill in them a sense of justice, brotherhood, and fidelity. (p. 91)

An education that is considerate of the poor will require that teachers learn to understand and be compassionate as well as stand in solidarity with the marginalized so they can interpret human reality from their perspective and pass this on to their students.

It is the task of school leaders to define a vision with accompanying goals and targets supportive of a broadened mission; monitor operations to conform with standards and directions emanating from the mission-vision; deploy resources in accordance with priorities; above all, develop personnel accordingly, and form a school culture that encourages and supports community members to succeed at their common vocation and adopt the shared Lasallian spirit of faith and zeal. Alpago (2004, p. 4) sees this culture in terms of the relationships among professionals with their students: "Among their colleagues, there is respect, openness, collaboration, solidarity, dialogue, mutual support, affection. . . . Towards their students, there is respect, valuing of persons, interest in individual situations, concern for their progress, readiness to adapt, availability, and creativity to make use of new pedagogical resources."

The Shared Mission

From the very beginning, De La Salle seemed to have known and practiced the shared mission. He made no distinctions between himself and the other Brothers, nor between the Brothers and lay partners. He saw all of them together as co-equal, co-responsible partners involved in the fulfillment of the school mission. When he made the historic vow of commitment to the mission together with twelve others in 1694, Rummery (2004, p. 4) states that those who took the vow did so out of preference, but it was clear that "the common mission was to be served by all, with or without vows." De La Salle allowed himself to be influenced by a layman, Adrien Nyel, in committing to what became the Lasallian mission. After he had established himself as an educational leader and the La Salle schools were negatively affected by the case brought against him by the writing masters, he chose to temporarily keep distance by going to the south of France, and there he, with a doctorate in theology, sought the advice of an unlettered laywoman, a shepherdess named Louise. Clearly, despite what he had achieved, De La Salle did not consider himself superior to a layperson. However, the dominant thinking and acting in the Church then propagated the leadership of a few versus the passivity of the majority, the paternalism of the clergy to the obedience of the laity. This must have somehow influenced the La Salle school communities as well because there was a time when laypersons merely assisted the Brothers in what was believed to be the mission only of the religious.

Botana (2004, p. 106) defines the shared mission as "a process of communion for the mission . . . of creating bonds that produce co-responsibility, which is the capacity to be in solidarity with the others, each according to his/(her) proper identity, in reaching the goals of a common project." The General Chapter of the Christian Brothers, an internationally participated assembly that reflects, discerns, visions, and plans long term for the Institute, officially declared in 1976 that the mission was henceforth shared with lay partners. This was affirmed and reaffirmed in even stronger terms by the succeeding General Chapters of 1986, 1993, and 2000. In fact, what used to be participated in only by Brothers included regionally selected partner representatives in 1993 and 2000. The 42nd General Chapter (1993) spoke of a reciprocal commitment to the shared mission involving partners and Brothers. The last General Chapter (2000) calls for a more widespread participation of representative partners in policy making relative to the Lasallian mission. Hence, the different International Commissions of the Christian Brothers Institute now include selected partners from every region, exercising voice and vote equal to those of the Brothers.

In his article "The Change of Age and Its Signs," Comte (2004, p. 5) states that "among current evolutions brought about by Vatican II . . . is the common condition of every Christian—that belonging to the People of God is more fundamental than any distinction of functions; and the reaffirmation that the call to holiness is not reserved to specialists."

Botana (2004) sees the Brothers and partners complementing one another in the fulfillment of mission in the same way:

> The Lasallian charism for Christian education is a gift that the Holy Spirit has given to the Church, not just to the Brothers, and this charism belongs to the lay as well. ... Both are protagonists and leaders responsible for the mission to complete its objectives. They are not substituting or replacing anyone; each one acts in accordance with his/(her) identity, some from consecrated celibacy, others from their experience of family life and reality of society. There are no tasks reserved only for Brothers but they share their sign of Brotherhood and experience of communion, of life dedicated to seeking God and His will, and gratuity in the free and total gift of self. ... Brothers and lay are together, not on opposite sides, but mutually complement each other and are in solidarity with one another. (p. 207)

All draw inspiration from De La Salle; all are committed to the same mission. And none of them can claim exclusive rights to the Lasallian heritage because it is now shared.

Current statistics show that about 96% of those in Lasallian schools and other ministries are not Brothers but partner sharers in the same Lasallian heritage and fruitfulness. The number of Brothers in the last ten years both professed and in formation shows a decreasing trend, including in the Asia Pacific region, even in the Philippines. On the other hand, the number of ministries and the number of clients served by these ministries continue to increase. A recent study on the "Viability and Vitality of the Lasallian Mission in the Asia Pacific Region" by Quebengco, Marco, and Luistro, FSC, shows that the ratio of Brothers to partners in schools is 1:54 or 1.84% Brothers, with the Philippines having the most lopsided ratio at 1:163 or only 0.61% Brothers. Even for practical reasons alone, the concept and practice of the shared mission make good sense, as the alternative is lesser, shrinking ministries due to lack of prepared, committed personnel that will diminish the impact of the Lasallian mission in the region.

Reading about the shared mission from articles and books written by Brothers and partners, and saying it is a practice whose time has come may intellectually be easy to agree with; however, from the perspectives and experience of those who live it on a daily basis, is the view the same? During the PARC 27 meeting of Brother Provincials and the Christian Brothers General Council in November 2003, Br. Armin Luistro, FSC, then Provincial of the Philippine district, listed and discussed the communication gap between Brothers and partners, the formation of partners for the mission, and the lack of clarity on Lasallian association membership, as among the concerns and challenges in the Asia Pacific region. Data from a survey conducted among the Brothers show that in the Asia Pacific region, 69% of Brothers (85% in the Philippines) believe that in ten years more partners will have to take over positions currently held by Brothers in Lasallian ministries. However, it is also perceived by 55% of Brothers in the Asia Pacific region (13% in the Philippines) that there is a lack of competent partners for the mission; and 49% of the same Brothers (45% in the Philippines) claim that partners do not understand the Lasallian mission well (Quebengco, Marco, Luistro, 2004, p. 48). The same study (p. 52) shows that while 60% of Brothers (78% in the Philippines) accept the concept and practice of the shared mission, their perception of partner acceptance of the same is even lower at 42% (75% in the Philippines). To the question of the desirability of partners taking over leadership positions from the Brothers in Lasallian ministries (p. 27), only 38% said yes (88% in the Philippines). The situation in the Philippines is very encouraging, although the acceptance of the practice of shared mission is still not 100%. This may be so because the Brothers also see their partners as competent and committed to the mission, though they all realize that partner formation for the mission is still needed. This is not the situation in the other Asia Pacific countries.

There is still much that can be done to be able to substantially and fully realize the shared mission. More partners need formation in understanding Lasallian tradition and concepts, as well as training for leadership roles. Comte (2004) sees another kind of obstacle to hurdle:

> In the coming years, both groups will have to learn to live in this new concept. The Brothers will have to accept those newcomers into the family without feeling that they have been dispossessed of

what they considered themselves as the only heirs. The lay people will have to find their full stature alongside the Brothers without being only a pale copy of them. We could ask if we are not all being called out of the logic of having (where each hangs on to what is considered his identity) in order to enter into a logic of gift (each considering to give and receive in return) as this is the best way to fully recognizing one another. (p. 3)

Lasallian Association

Although there are Brothers and partners who see the necessity of more work to be done to make the shared mission a significant reality, there are also many who have exhibited not only competence and commitment to the shared mission, they have organized themselves voluntarily into living communities for a particular mission. As such, they also voluntarily give up certain freedoms in life for the mission. Examples of this are religious communities such as the Christian Brothers and the Hermanas Guadalupanas, Lasallian partner communities such as the Lasallian Volunteers, and more recently, the Alternativity Community. This is not a convenient living-together arrangement, but living together as a Lasallian community for a specific mission. There are other Lasallians all over the world whose commitment to the mission is no less intense, and who wish to do the same. The experience particularly of partners, who now do so, will be valuable for others to be encouraged, be inspired, and follow.

There are partners who have asked whether there ought to be formally recognized Lasallian associations and associates in addition to the partners among those ready and willing to commit to the Lasallian mission for life. Although sharing the mission is possible without being associated or becoming an associate, to be associated or become an associate will require sharing the mission. As Botana (2004, p. 115) explained, "The process of the shared mission gives rise to the Lasallian association and is the hinge upon which the whole process turns. . . . It is a bond of solidarity between persons for a mission and for that matter makes them interdependent." Comte (2004, p. 7) adds, "Association is a central reality in our tradition. It could be a response to the desire for belonging, manifested today among many people. Would it not be interesting to show this belonging particularly in showing it as normally, the fruit of a common construction ... where Lasallian identity is the fruit of a community journey, directed towards an objective." The object is not collegiality or friendship among associates, though those will most likely be present; neither is it membership in an "elite" group, but to share the mission, deepen commitment to it, and convert this into a lifelong journey. Association is a further development or a much deeper form of partnership for both the mission and the persons involved, be they sharer-associates or those being served.

The Brothers have encouraged this development, and Comte (2004, p. 6) expresses this: "After introducing lay people to the Lasallian tradition, there must come a phase where they will be the authors of a new expression of this tradition. They must not be placed simply in a position of being repeaters."

The 43rd General Chapter of the Christian Brothers in 2000 describes the development from partnership to being associated for the mission in this manner:

> There are partners who have a long record of collaborating in the Lasallian mission and who feel a call to deepen the charism's spirituality and Lasallian commitment in which they wish to participate. In particular, their lives are already marked by a number of distinctly Lasallian characteristics:
>
> - a vocation inspired by the charism of St. La Salle and his values
>
> - a life of faith which discovers God in everyday life understood in the light of scripture, and for persons of other religions, in the light of their own sacred text
>
> - a community experience of some form or other suited to the identity of its members

- a mission of some duration which associates persons with the educational service of the poor

- an openness of mind which makes it possible to see beyond the individual and his immediate environment

(p. 4)

As a follow up to this, the Superior General and his Council constituted an International Commission on Association, composed of Brothers and partners representing their respective regions, to further conceptualize, clarify, and refine; lay down the foundation and guiding principles that will govern Lasallian associations; and, possibly, the conferral of associate status, based on Lasallian tradition, current realities, and the relevant experience of Lasallian regions and districts. Considering the variation in culture and stages of development among them, the work is immensely challenging.

Six commissioned studies have been conducted to shed more light on Lasallian associations, which serve as inputs in the discussions and discernment of the commission. There are also issues to be tackled, such as whether or not to formalize the conferment of associates as this may lead to some form of elitism and prove divisive to a district; what criteria will be used in a district's official recognition of associations and/or associates; what guidelines would be fair and acceptable considering the unique characteristics and features of every district, etc. Comte (2004) admits:

> We are still in an experimental phase in what concerns our association with lay people. Exchanging experiences—directly or indirectly—could stimulate us. What we could never imagine is being done elsewhere. What has been lived in a certain part of the Institute could focus our attention on the paths of the future or show us difficulties and dead ends. (p. 6)

Hence, consultations with the different districts are currently being conducted with respect to their experiences of the shared mission and association. On the basis of these, the Commission will prepare the working draft of a paper on Lasallian association for presentation to an international meeting of Brothers and partners in 2006. Based on the feedback gathered there, the revised draft will be made for presentation to the Superior General and his Council. From there, it will be presented to the Christian Brothers General Chapter in 2007 for further deliberations and, hopefully, approval. In the meantime the work of the Commission goes on.

Considering that there are currently sixty-six Lasallian ministries in the Philippine district catering to 100,725 students and beneficiaries, serviced by 6,500 partners and about forty Brothers, the effective implementation of the Lasallian shared mission and association can make a real difference in the lives of so many, and serve as a potent force in making a significant impact to Philippine development. That can be the Lasallians' best gift to the nation!

This article was first published by the Lasallian Institute for Development and Research, College of Education, De La Salle University-Manila, in a collection of essays titled "Visions for Education: Essays on Philippine Education in Honor of Br. Andrew Gonzalez, FSC," 2005.

Author Biography

Carmelita Quebengco is the executive vice president for De La Salle University-Manila (Philippines). As a professor and University Fellow at De La Salle University, she has extensive involvement in trustee boards of Lasallian institutions across the Philippines. She is a frequent contributor to higher educational conferences and she volunteers as project director for the Development of a Philippine Center for Tribal Education and the Pundasyon Hanunuo Mangyan School Project.

Bibliography

Alpago, Bruno, FSC. "The Challenge of Belonging." Brothers of the Christian Schools. Rome. April 2004.

Botana, Antonio, FSC. "The Educators' Life Journey." MEL Bulletin 8/9. Brothers of the Christian Schools. Rome. March 2004.

Comte, Robert, FSC. "The Change of Age and Its Signs." Brothers of the Christian Schools. Rome. April 2004.

———. "Lasallian Identity Today: A Differentiated Identity." Brothers of the Christian Schools. Rome. April 2004.

Fitzpatrick, Edward, FSC. *La Salle: Patron of All Teachers*. The Bruce Publishing Company. Milwaukee. 1951.

Gil, Pedro, FSC. "The Challenge of Mission: Reinventing the Educational Community." Brothers of the Christian Schools. Rome. April 2004.

Luistro, Armin, FSC. Report to PARC 27. November 2003.

Meister, Michael, FSC. "Lasallian Spirituality and Association." Brothers of the Christian Schools. Rome. April 2004.

Quebengco, C., Marco, J., Luistro, A., FSC. "The Viability and Vitality of PARC Sectors." PARC. January 2005.

Rummery, G., FSC. "The Journey of the Lasallian Community." Brothers of the Christian Schools. Rome. April 2004.

Van Grieken, George, FSC. *Touching the Heart of Students*. Christian Brothers Publications. Maryland. 1999.

LASALLIAN UNIVERSITIES: A RISING STAR

By: Philippe M. Choquet

Introduction

Created in 1854, the Superior Agricultural Institute of Beauvais (ISAB) is one of the oldest institutions of higher education in the Lasallian system. Confronted with the higher education revolution in France as well as in Europe, the Brothers and leaders understood that the strength of the ISAB lay in its Lasallian roots and history. Recently we discovered a Lasallian university network, thanks to the International Association of Lasallian Universities (IALU). Even though ISAB has belonged to various secular networks for some time, we decided that the institution should become completely involved in the Lasallian system. This was a strategic decision that was reflected in our decision to change the institution's name to La Salle Beauvais Polytechnic Institute. Our decision to do so is based on the exciting evolution of higher education, a field to which ISAB can humbly contribute.

In order to understand the strategic vision of ISAB regarding the future of Lasallian higher education, I propose to address three issues:

- Goals and Mission: does the Lasallian educational project really respond to society's expectations?

- Analysis of the external environment: threats and opportunities, strengths and weaknesses related to higher education.

- Development of a strategy for Lasallian universities, not only for each university, but also for the network.

I will finish this essay with a reflection about the theme: Lasallian universities and agricultural teaching as a way to eliminate poverty from its roots.

I. Lasallian Universities: Are they an answer to society's expectations?

Our universities are inspired by a social sense of the Lasallian mission to educate youth. Therefore, the question of the sense of the Lasallian mission is essential and preliminary to every strategic consideration. In the context of the suburban crisis that shook France on various occasions in the autumn of 2005, I had the opportunity to present a Lasallian educational project to different politicians with diverse responsibilities: economic, university, etc. Surprisingly, this educational project seemed to be the appropriate answer to the educational problems underlying this serious crisis: to develop a sense of respect, the sense of compromise and service, contrary to individualism, to fight against the inequality of our society.

The work of Saint John Baptist de La Salle, throughout its three hundred years, seems more appropriate now than ever. It responds to the deep needs of our society. Notwithstanding, it is necessary to verify if it meets the expectations of our "clients": the students, the parents, and the future employers.

Youth often come to the university with ideals of equality, justice, altruism. However, as soon as they immerse themselves into professional life, these ideals are frequently substituted by materialistic or even individualistic ends. What happens between the ages of 18 and 25? What is the responsibility of our universities so that these young people can acquire solid values, capable of resisting society's worldly pressure? Our students are morally hungry and are waiting for us to nourish their hunger for altruism with something that is structured and that will constitute a beneficial engine in their lives.

Additionally, youth expect our university message to resonate with them as it inspires the unity and dynamism of the group. The best picture of this is the remarkable mobilization of the students in the demonstrations concerning humanity. As an example, one can cite the Ovalies tournament organized every year by the students of ISAB. Launched in 1955, this humanitarian effort has become a premier European university rugby tournament. In 2006, eighty teams of rugby with 1,300 participants donated 20,000€ to Médicins Sans Frontiers (Doctors Without Borders). This was a generous manifestation of kindness and it has become the motor issue of ISAB. In 2006, the Ovalies was elected the Best Student Association 2006 at the French level.

Parental encounters with learning institutions are stronger and more frequent. This is especially true in primary and secondary education, and is becoming more evident in higher education. In fact, matriculation into a university often corresponds to a moment of anxiety not only for the young but also for the parents. This uneasiness, more or less justified, is related to the child's maturity. In fact, the "post adolescent" students, between 17 and 18 years, have an advantage over mature adults. Parents are assisted greatly in this transition by recognizing that their child will be studying in a structured environment, marked with firm educational objectives. To this end, Lasallian educational works, well adapted to higher education, seem to respond positively to parents' expectations.

From the perspective of the business world, one would think the chief expectation of universities is that graduates have technically functional capabilities. In a surprising way, interviewing the managers of different companies (regardless of whether they were Lasallian alumni or not), their replies were consistent: youth entering the labor market are reflections of society at large. This is to say, they exhibit individualized tendencies, lack collaborative tendencies, and fail to exhibit volunteerism or the capacity to work together. Understandably, the expectation of business leaders is increasingly more technical (for whom the university credentials are sufficient guarantee of quality). Nevertheless, they also are desirous of seeing humanistic qualities, a capacity to assume responsibility, to work together with others, and to be leaders within a group. These are Lasallian values. When one fights against poverty, a matter about which business leaders are increasingly sensitive, they consider issues of lasting development. They have the ability to incorporate the economic realities of their enterprise in doing so. The speech organized for the 150th anniversary of ISAB had the theme "Enterprises: What are the values you are looking for?" From this, it is clearly seen that the economic world is seeking values and that Lasallian educational works can contribute to the development of strong environmental values.

In conclusion, the Lasallian educational project of Lasallian universities seems to respond perfectly to the demands of the youth, their parents, and the future employers. The Lasallian mission makes sense in the higher education universe as it serves both society and youth.

II. Strategic Challenges for Lasallian Universities

For a number of years, the higher educational and research sectors have been subject to increasingly dynamic competition. In order to visualize the strategic perspectives of the Lasallian university network, it is essential, above all, to understand the context, to analyze the threats and opportunities that are present in our institutions, and to understand both forces and relative weaknesses.

In terms of threats and opportunities, the primary galvanizing issue is the phenomenon of globalization: economic globalization, enterprise globalization, globalization of the academic diploma norms, and student international mobility. National higher education is in the process of quickly moving toward internationalization due to increased competition. Those who consider higher education as a business activity will sharpen their appetite for this globalization and integrate higher education in the negotiations of the World Commerce Organization.

Viewing things broadly, the macroeconomic indicators suggest that the "market" seems promising:

- The need for academic competencies is more and more important in research.

- The world population is growing, especially in the developing countries where the need, in terms of education, is enormous.

- The states, after the Johannesburg Summit in 2002, have decided, as a goal, to provide education to the whole population, giving priority to elementary education. Therefore, they have "diminished" higher education because it is too expensive to develop, and they have let the private sector respond to this increasing demand. As such, it will experience an important increase in the years ahead.

As a consequence, globalization presents developmental opportunities that must be satisfied.

The strengthening of these factors will yield some market differentiation in such a manner as to reduce costs. Among the more notable differentiation elements one might cite are academic excellence (attraction, rejection rate, work study); quality in research; quality in educational instruction; and strong relationships with desirable business placements. The manner in which these elements are synthesized will determine the market difference, thus allowing institutions to build a strong brand.

Parallel to differential strategies, universities can have volume/cost strategies, allowing competitive advantages to be built on a price-distribution level. Functions that are most sensitive to the effects of size include but are not limited to research, marketing, international relations, and lobbying. Functions that are more sensitive in terms of size include teaching (possibility to offer courses with a large choice of options) and the relations with the economic world. Functions that are less sensitive in terms of capacity include education and educational projects.

Because of such sensitivity and its long-term effects, many universities have established growth strategies, internal development (when it is possible), external procurement (buying schools, bringing together departments, acquiring new schools), or forming alliances and consortia that link international development with the creation of affiliates.

In this new context, all the universities, including those that are well known, are exposed to the risks of competition. In turn, to make progress they need to develop themselves or reengineer in order to guarantee their existence. According to Darwin's law, under an environment of constant change, only those who best know how to adapt themselves will survive. Accordingly, it is certain that private enterprises, such as Lasallian universities, are better prepared and more capable of adapting to changes than the public universities. There are numerous reasons for this:

- Their inherent organizational form and decision-making systems.

- Their financial autonomy (as it appears as a feasible fact in the public universities) that allows them to maneuver margins in terms of investment, differing from state universities because the international development does not generally enter in the goals and are nowadays confronted with drastic budgets.

- The capacity to form alliances or ties with institutions and administer cultural differences.

It is encouraging that Lasallian universities have reinforced the private sector thanks to the initiative of IALU and the strength of "Through Association." In effect:

- This is essentially a global network (65 universities on 4 continents).

- It consists of institutions that share the same educational orientation and that are born from the influence of Saint John Baptist de La Salle. All demonstrate the same rigor, academic pragmatism, and culture. Students transferring from one university to another can substantiate this claim.

- It is functional. For example, the Brothers of the Christian Schools have a major structural advantage with regard to formation. IALU has enabled exchanges between diverse universities thanks to the notable *Encuentros* among presidents and annual thematic meetings in Cuernavaca.

- It is a network that develops and gives proof to the Lasallian universities around the world.

- "La Salle" is a strong brand name worldwide thanks to the international coordination of schools (from elementary to higher).

This dynamic network helps us triumph over any individual or collective disabilities by our collaboration "together and by association." A high degree of cooperation exists between and among institutions.

III. LaSalle Universities' Strategies: Reinforcement and Development

As mentioned before, the Lasallian universities network is a successful lever of change for each one of our institutions and assists them in becoming a successful group dedicated to service for mission. In this context, it is necessary to constantly reinforce and redevelop the capacity to follow faithfully the mission of Saint Jean Baptist de La Salle in higher education.

III-1. To Continue Reinforcing the IALU Network

The benefit derived as a result of our network should permit Lasallian universities to differentiate themselves from others based on "quality." Listed below are some university activities where cooperation among network members would seem beneficial.

Teaching

One of the things that makes our universities thematically similar is their dedication to teaching as a primary function of education. Logically, synergies in this area are possible with the end result being to better our programs in the following manner:

- By benchmarking with innovative pedagogies.

- By "academic hybridizing" existing programs to increase the value students receive. One could cite several examples: the use of videoconferences (our universities at Barcelona and Bajio have already done this successfully); the La Salle project online that has created a database and a series of the online courses and case studies; the opportunity to take elective courses or complementary specializations among cooperating universities; the possibility of obtaining diplomas from cooperating institutions.

- To arrive at this level of academic integration, it is essential that faculty exchange programs be developed among universities, just as we already have student exchanges.

- To have a common desire to increase the levels of research and teaching. In order to achieve this, we will need to make a priority of our use of informational technology in teaching and research.

Research

Research is not the primary mission of the Lasallian schools; instead our faculties are oriented toward the education of the young. However, at the university level, research is necessary and often considered a symbol of academic excellence. In distinction to public universities, research at Lasallian universities is not an end in itself but a means: by forming the students for investigations, research also serves as a means of updating the professor's knowledge. It establishes strong professional ties with colleagues, and in doing so, benefits the students, the professors, and society in general. Realizing that financial support is often limited, research is, without doubt, a weakness of our universities. We must address this issue if we are to achieve academic excellence. The Lasallian network can assist in this development by sharing resources and announcing the availability of existing experts, available research opportunities, entrepreneurial contacts, and research interests of universities in the system.

On the other hand, research with public finances should be made a priority for the network: lobbying, permissible contests, relations with multinationals, etc.

International Relations

The internalization of universities and their campuses will become a key element for their academic recognition in years to come. As in any enterprise, it is important for students to have an appreciation for international relations in order to secure global positions in the workforce. The Lasallian network will have to boost the internationalization of our universities:

- for recruiting: from secondary to higher, from BSc to MSc

- for the mobilization of students among courses

- for professors and employees

Importantly, these exchanges are the means to make our association effective and alive and to reinforce/cultivate the Lasallian spirit, a strategic starting point for establishing a community of Brothers.

Educational Project

Considering that our institutions all have historic origins in the "Conduct of Schools" as authored by Saint John Baptist de La Salle, they share a common heritage and appropriately adapt themselves to each level of teaching. While Lasallian universities are not as geographically numerous as primary and secondary Lasallian schools, the good work in Mexican and Philippine higher educational systems should serve as international models for other countries to increase their national density of university institutions.

Marketing

As we have seen previously, marketing is an important element in the design of universities. It is clear that the collective capitalization under the brand name "La Salle" is something fundamentally important. Thus, the decision taken by university presidents in the Barcelona 2004 *Encuentro* to evolve toward "La Salle" recognition internationally is a prudent strategic initiative. With some timidity but with great vision, former students at the 150-year-old ISAB changed our institutional name to La Salle Beauvais Polytechnic Institute because strategically—in both the long and short run—this marketing choice is the most rational decision.

A strongly established brand that is defended collectively on a global scale will help strengthen connections with students (initial marketing) as well as with enterprises (later marketing). Already, joint initiatives have been undertaken, such as the collaboration of La Salle University Barcelona and ISAB in marketing their MSc degree in South America, China, and India, as well as with Christian Brothers University (Memphis, TN, USA) in the MSc in engineering management.

The IALU network can serve to stimulate relationships with multinational enterprises, assist with international contracts, and encourage commercial development and connections among other networks of former students.

These different marketing activities should help to reinforce the value of the brand and increase the notoriety of Lasallian universities. Such activities will require lobbying to promote our vision of youth education around the world, and additionally provide opportunities for businesses to assist financially with the development of our schools.

III-2. Developing the Lasallian University Network

In developing the Lasallian university network, we need to be sensitive to two objectives: (1) how to strengthen existing higher educational institutions, and (2) how to follow the missionary work of De La Salle by responding to the higher educational needs of various countries, especially underdeveloped areas.

The IALU network can be a catalyst of internal growth for existing universities by creating new courses, transferring existing programs (for example between La Salle in Barcelona and La Salle in Bajio), and by establishing new programs among member universities (such as the recently developed masters in business administration). The development of a degree program in environmental education might be an excellent way to begin this kind of global cooperation among Lasallian universities. Through such action, our schools might be able to increase the number of matriculated students, particularly those from outside the country, and by doing so, reinforce the international collective marketing of the Lasallian network.

As previously mentioned, there are more opportunities than ever to develop favorable IALU contacts in developing new universities. To accomplish this, it will be necessary to mobilize human and financial resources. On many levels, Lasallian universities can contribute to one another, ensuring there is pedagogical transfer of information.

The creation of new Lasallian universities can be accomplished: in countries where Lasallian universities currently exist (new establishments or through the absorption of previously existing universities); in countries where the De La Salle Brothers are present, with the help of secondary institutions (such as in the Mediterranean area and India); or, in the countries where the De La Salle Brothers are not yet present but where strategically it would be important for the betterment of the IALU network and the Lasallian mission (such as Eastern Europe, China, and Southeast Asia).

In considering higher education around the world, one must not forget the challenges of gaining access to African higher education. Without this access, individuals experience sociological, economic, and political handicaps. This zone is unsettled, and the development of higher education should be developed in coordination with IALU and the assistance of international agencies (UNESCO, World Bank, financing from UE or USA, etc.).

In conclusion, the needs are enormous. Lasallian higher education is responding to the true needs of our society today; it needs to continue this trend in the future, particularly in developing countries. With a missionary spirit, we should respond to the "call" to continue the work of Saint John Baptist de La Salle and his first Brothers. Together and by association we can respond to this growthful opportunity.

IV. Lasallian Universities and Agricultural Education: A Means to Attack the Causes of Poverty?

IV-1. Current Situation

ISAB activities were originally focused on the agronomical sciences and agricultural management. Later, the school diversified to include agricultural nutrition, environmental science, and marketing, thus addressing the necessary competences to develop a rural world. In the IALU network, very few universities (less than 10 of the 65 members) are strongly positioned on the agricultural and agricultural nutrition themes. The reasons are various:

- The majority of Lasallian universities teach primarily the liberal arts and engineering.

- Specialized agricultural higher educational needs are often covered by public universities which capably address agricultural issues and programs.

- The socioeconomic level of farmers in developing countries is relatively low; this financial situation acts as a disincentive for study in the agricultural sciences.

IV-2. The Fight Against Rural Exodus Root of Urban Poverty: A Challenge of the 21st Century

Many developing countries, such as those throughout the Mediterranean, South America, Southeast Asia, China, and India, are in an important growth transition. Their fragility is due to a great abyss that exists between rich and poor, especially in rural and urban zones. This economic divide has yielded a massive exodus from rural areas; farmers who lack sufficient income leave the countryside in hope of a better life in the city. Unfortunately, this population inflates the city's urban surroundings and their poverty is transformed into misery.

The control of this rural exodus is a great challenge for developing countries, noticeably China and India. The fight against poverty in rural zones is the best way to limit this urban flight and the concomitant misery that results. If countries could organize better marketing opportunities for rural products, develop small agricultural food enterprises, and create added value, farmers would stay in the countryside. This would help to break this unfortunate rural flight to urban poverty.

Perhaps lessons from the past might be instructive. In 1854, France experienced an industrial revolution. The Brothers of that time sought to fight against poverty. In doing so, they had the idea of creating an educational agricultural school, the ISAB, to form farmers that would be leaders in their environment. On a technical level, they could improve farmers' profits. On a professional level, they could form an organization to improve affiliated agricultural structures. The former students of ISAB, filled with the Lasallian spirit, contributed mightily to the development of agriculture in France. They enhanced the agricultural nutritional structure and, more generally, contributed positively to the dynamic nature of French rural zones.

IV-3. An IALU Agricultural Network to Fight Against the Causes of Poverty

If the Lasallian university network desired to help act upon poverty, especially in countries with a large agricultural population, it could assist in the formation of leaders and entrepreneurs for the economic activity in rural zones where there is agriculture.

It was in this spirit that the first meeting of an IALU thematic subgroup gathered together Lasallian universities that have agricultural programs (Mexico, Colombia, France, and Brazil). This subgroup has the possibility of making contact with other universities that are dealing with agriculture. This group hopes that other Lasallian universities will be interested in an economic development of the rural world, and would partner with us in preventing an endemic cycle of poverty.

In addition to this agricultural/nutritional entrepreneur thematic in rural zones, other themes related to the rural world are also essential and need to be considered, including (a) the problem of adequate nutrition and health on a global scale, and (b) environmental issues such as pollution, water access, health risks, and the proper administration of natural resources.

Our society's agricultural issues are linked to the issues and challenges of poverty. One focus of the Lasallian university network might be to help develop viable solutions to these vexing problems of humanity.

Author Biography

Philippe Choquet serves as the executive president of Institute Polytechnique LaSalle Beauvais (Instiut Supérieur d'Agriculture de Beauvais-France), after coming to education from corporate experience with Peri-G consulting and Semillas Verneuil, S.A., Cordoba, Spain. His advanced degrees are from the Institut Supérieur d'Agriculture de Beauvais and the London Business School.

THE LASALLIAN MISSION TODAY:
PERSPECTIVES FROM THE MAIN POINTS OF THE
LASALLIAN LATIN AMERICAN REGIONAL EDUCATION
PROJECT (PERLA)

By: Carlos G. Gómez Restrepo, FSC

Introduction

Fellow Lasallians in Latin America have reflected significantly on the role of education in our society. In fact, there is an awareness of a great wealth that can be found in many of our countries. This wealth is represented by human capital in the form of young people that give us hope for the future, by abundant resources and by the constant search for enhanced possibilities. On the other hand, we also recognize the difficult living situations the Continent experiences: poverty, violence, exclusion, the fragility of our democracies, and the unjust distribution of wealth.

The Lasallian Latin American Educational Project—PERLA for its initials in Spanish (Relal, 2001)—identifies, as a starting point, the need to be more meaningfully directed in the sociopolitical context where Lasallians are present—to choose to keep some things and give up other things that remain behind. Institutional reflections in the last few years demand new commitments and new presences to address educational needs. This implies that one cannot continue indifferent political positions when the fate of the poor rests in a world in which few care. Thus, this project is founded on five principle points: the explicit proclamation of the Gospel; the democratization of knowledge; sustainable human development; the promotion of justice, peace, and the right to life; and the defense of the Rights of the Child. As Br. Álvaro Rodríguez, current Superior General of the Institute, said, "Our Institute was born on the fringes of dehumanization" (2001), and today we are perplexed by another process of dehumanization with similar shades but different contexts and realities from the process that gave birth to the foundation of the Institute. Perhaps this may be the scenario where the recasting of the Lasallian university mission becomes a reality.

Besides the defined elements that are essential to an educational project, it is also necessary to reflect on the specificity of a particular project. In this case, in addition to responding to the reality of Latin America and the world as well as to the anthropological challenges of youth, it is necessary to reflect on what Lasallianism contributes with regard to its specificity, tradition, educational style, pedagogy, and vision of the mission, of the teacher, of the school, etc. In other words, the question is, "What is distinct and distinctive about the PERLA project with respect to other educational projects?" The answers are multiple: first, the dialogue with other groups and projects; second, the certain knowledge of what we offer and why people can look to us in the future; third, the realization that we can assume solid, daring, and prophetic positions because we have the clarity of the what, how, and why; and fourth, it gives us a secure path as to how we should form our Brothers, associates, and lay partners and even proposes a framework of reference for our universities and, particularly, our schools of education.

Lasallian higher education has expanded significantly in Latin America. Today there are thirty-five institutions in eleven countries in the region. We feel the need to articulate our own thinking so as to serve as inspiration for our universities. It hasn't been easy, perhaps because as Lasallians, we are better "doers" than "thinkers." But that does not excuse us from the historical responsibility we assume once we have decided to establish ministries in higher education.

Brother Rodríguez, addressing the Lasallian Latin American universities, said:

> We lack the concrete ties and practical connections that will allow us
> to function as a unified network motivated by the same vision and
> passion for the dream of the kingdom of our Father. "His work" is "our

work" De La Salle often said and together we are making Latin America "the work of God." You have the spaces of dialogue that no other works, children, or young people have. You can support all the projects of the region, by making the whole group of actors more professional, by better preparing educators, by generating new research, presenting new alternatives, by helping them find the financial resources that would permit them to better function to benefit the poor and marginalized of the Continent, in short, by interacting more generously with the whole Lasallian educational system. (2003)

Today it is known that the Lasallian university must have a significant presence in our society and its educational offering must be clear in its intentions. The university should be explicit in its options that inspire the creation and offering of academic programs, university extension projects, lines of investigation, and pedagogical reflections. And, because of the complexity of today's world and due to the historical importance the university has in the modeling and proposals for a new society, the university must also assume other functions as its own: the *political function* that obliges the Lasallian university to be proactive in its proposals, daring in its positions, and incisive in the formulation of public policies and development plans, and not to be merely reactive to the decisions of others or where its presence might have been possible through debate, research, and the integral proposal of projects; the *ethical function* that situates the university as part of the moral conscience of a country; and the *systematic function* that impels it to articulate itself with other social actors and in a specific way with the educational continuum.

The main points of the PERLA are, without a doubt, a source of inspiration of the Lasallian university mission. Let us see how and why.

Explicit Proclamation of the Gospel

The Founder was an intellectual Catholic committed to the transformation of society in his times. He had the possibility of access to the highest level of education in the seventeenth century and obtained his doctorate in theology. His written works testify to his concerns and "lines of research," where he joined together his theoretical and scientific reflections with a faith put to the test and a committed public practice to the unfortunate, which brought him persecution from both the guild of educators of that time and the civil and ecclesiastical powers of the time. In the imagination of De La Salle, faith and science, culture and the gospel, commitment with education and service to society were inseparable.

How do we make this vision of higher education of the Founder come true? Undoubtedly the Lasallian university inspiration carries with it as the primary goal the promotion of the evangelization of culture, the ministry of the intelligence in the context of science, culture, reason, faith, as well as the identity and leadership of the Catholic intellectual as the committed layperson in the construction of the country. Any university is Lasallian if, in addition to educating in our values, it fosters, among others and without excluding individuals, educational communities of intellectual Catholics. Thus, three strategic lines of search and action for the explicit proclamation of the Gospel appear in the Lasallian university: to promote the evangelization of culture, to promote the ministry of intelligence, and to promote the identity and leadership of the Catholic intellectual.

The Latin American Church has been emphatic in the educational responsibility of the Church and especially of the university. The Conference of Santo Domingo proposes a great pastoral challenge:

> The Catholic university—the university of Christian inspiration—is a great challenge, given that its role is especially one of realizing the Christian project of man and, therefore, it has to be in a lively, continuous and progressive dialogue with humanism and the culture of technology, such that it knows how to teach the true Christian wisdom in which the model of the "working man," combined with that of the "wise man," culminates in Jesus Christ. (1992, no. 268)

The Lasallian university must create spaces for a fertile dialogue of science and cultures, reason and faith, gospel and society. These intentional spaces welcome both the educational processes of the faculty and their investigations. As a result, their efforts should engage options that touch the very concept of the human being, the model of society, the economic model, the strengthening of democracy, and so on.

The Lasallian university as a pastoral environment is based on a fundamental strategy to propose the following of Christ to the generations of young people looking to be educated at a higher level and for a higher level. To practice vanguard leadership in the ministry of the intelligence in this place of the creation of science and culture is fundamental, given that the Lasallian university must proclaim the Gospel. The Superior General of the Brothers was very clear when he expressed the following:

> Our universities must be places where the Gospel is life and can be transmitted as a message and as a dialogue. Today's world needs more than theories, testimonies and signs to dismantle it and open it to transcendence. To that effect we can ask: What is the concept of evangelization at work in our universities? Do we offer a scale of alternative values, criticism to the status quo, an inspiring model for a society inspired by the values of the Gospel? Do our projects open to a transcendent horizon that allows everyone to live with respect and tolerance of pluralism and respect for the culture of the most fragile groups? To what degree do we offer clues to this spiritual search? (Rodríguez, 2004)

In a university it is the intellectuals who are the privileged agents of the implementation of these means. And in a Catholic university, more so in the Lasallian university, it is the intellectuals who are called to contribute. We can ask ourselves, "Who are the intellectuals?" They are the creators, interpreters, and communicators of knowledge and culture, the articulators of the symbolic world of people. Their fundamental task is to exercise as their main and permanent activity, teaching, investigation, the production of knowledge, the production of opinion, the modeling of culture, and, of course, its political impact, which is understood to mean as a reflection and commitment about what is public.

Given the character of the first line of its role, the Lasallian university must seriously formulate a policy of formation, amplification, and renovation of its intellectual elites and those in every country where it is located. This is especially important today in the context of the rapid internationalization of knowledge and technology.

Catholic Lasallian intellectuals present in our universities should exercise a triple function: the critical function, the expertise function, and the commitment function. The *critical* function requires the historical task of being a critical conscience of one's time and society. To be a Catholic intellectual is to be conscious of one's human context, using his capacity as a critic of political, economic, and spiritual powers, inspired in the Gospel. The function of *expertise* means that he is competent in knowing how to think and use his knowledge ethically and in the service of the poorest in his country. And finally, the function of *commitment* recuperates all its meaning in the description of "committed intellectual," an existential position through which he is connected and transforms the practices and relations of the powers of society in which he is immersed (Coronado, 2005).

In the Lasallian university, the explicit proclamation of the Gospel becomes the work of the Catholic intellectuals who are committed to it. They use scientific knowledge to transform societies. Any strategy of evangelization of culture and the ministry of the intelligence cannot be far removed from life or the commitment to what is human.

Democratization of Knowledge

In a world where the majority of people are poor, the Lasallian university is that much more Lasallian when its research begins and ends with a commitment of assistance to the poorest in the country. The idea is to think about the accessibility of the poorest to our universities and the impact our universities make in advancing popular educational projects. Mere talk about Lasallian higher education is nothing if we do not support that conversation with actions that demonstrate we are committed to the poorest in our countries.

The challenging question arises then: How can our universities carry out the "preferential option for the poorest" and the "together and by association educational service to the poor"?

Impressed with the reality of his times, De La Salle let himself be guided by the Holy Spirit in such a way that one commitment led to another. In that way, he responded creatively to the needs of the poor. Today the Lasallian university must favor its commitment to the poorest and most helpless of society, by making it the direct objective of the educational services and the formative and academic direction of the university (PID, 2003). If there is something that sets the Latin American Lasallian university apart, it is its preference for the poorest. We can ask ourselves again: What does favoring the poor mean for the university? We can contribute the following three insights:

- Poverty, understood as the lack of worldly goods, is in itself an evil. Poverty is not a condition desired by God, since it is the fruit of injustice. From this perspective, the option of the Lasallian university to give preferential treatment to the poor is carried out in the fight to overcome the unjust conditions of poverty and of economic, political, social, and cultural depravity in our communities.

- Poverty, seen as the commitment to and solidarity with the needy of this world—the poorest—implies a challenge to our university to go out to meet it on its own turf, to get close to it in order to know and study the reality of poverty, and to propose, through science and knowledge, alternatives to surmount it.

- Poverty, when seen as poor in spirit, describes those who value the goods of the world yet are not attached to them. They recognize the superior value of the goods of the Kingdom, giving rise in them to the readiness and gratitude of one who expects all things of the Lord and bends to his will. Based on this interpretation, it is then up to the Lasallian university to adopt an attitude of freedom when faced with worldly riches and share them with everyone, especially the most needy. We should use them with simplicity and moderation. It means having the goods and riches of this world not as an absolute but as a means, as a gift from the Lord to all so that they may reach their full potential. These goods must be shared fairly. It challenges the Catholic Lasallian intellectuals to a mysticism and spirituality that springs from the intellectual labor that made them become wise in the biblical sense (the beginning of all wisdom is the recognition of the action of the Lord), the action of one's own life and history, discovering as the Psalms say, "Great are the works of the Lord, worthy of the study of those who love them."

As institutions that create culture and knowledge, Lasallian universities must fight so that knowledge and culture reach the poorest. The Lasallian university positions people, science, and technology at the service of the poor. This can be seen on three levels: the level of assistance and beneficence, the level of promotion and human development, and the structural-transforming level.

The *assistance and beneficence* level is where the Lasallian universities practice charity and operational love with activities that are of immediate benefit, of aid to the needs and deficiencies of the people that cannot wait (such as hunger, sickness, natural disasters, etc.). Such action is inspired by the Bible: "Don't turn away from any of the poor" (Tb 4,8); "Refuse no one the good on which he has a claim" (Prv 3,27); "Come, you who are blessed by my Father. Inherit the kingdom prepared for you from the foundation of the world. For I was hungry and you gave me food, I was thirsty and you gave me drink, a stranger and you welcomed me, naked and you clothed me, ill and you cared for me, in prison and you visited me.... Whatever you did for one of these least brothers of mine, you did for me" (Mt 25,31–41).

The level of *promotion and human development,* through which the Lasallian university makes an effort to present the Gospel to the levels of the population without hope, brings them closer to the Word of God, so that they can feel that they are a living part of the Church, by making the poor protagonists in their own development. In order to do that, universities can facilitate conditions of well-being and enhanced quality of life by interdisciplinary intervention in urban communities or depressed rural sectors, through community organizations, and through the creation of microbusinesses, urbanization, education, health, etc.

The *structural-transforming* level, which is characteristic of universities, is the means by which they give structural answers to important social problems. It is political love and social charity brought to life through community organization and self-determination. Here is where the huge possibilities of committed Lasallian actions in the areas of ethics, mysticism, and politics come into play. As a result, the distinctive sign of the Lasallian university is its work for the promotion of justice and human rights. With this understanding, people, science, and technology are at the service of the poorest in our countries (Coronado, 2005).

Sustainable Human Development

Many of the perspectives used in the study of the social and economic phenomena of the twentieth century were supported by the need for "development." This understanding supported the idea of progress, from economic growth and scientific advances to even the option of a system of political organization. They were well known, especially in Latin America: ideological focuses such as "developmentalism" and programs of social aid such as "Alliance for Progress." Basically, an allusion was made to an idea of linear development, noted more for the economic growth than for its real effect on the living conditions of the populations. Upon closer inspection, these approximations were insufficient.

The United Nations Development Program (UNDP) has been one of the principal promoters of the new meaning of the concept. Since 1990, the annual report on development has gradually included and broadened its meaning. Finally, in 1994 it said that

> sustainable human development implies that the human being is placed in the center of the development process and that the activities of the present generations will not reduce the opportunities and the options of subsequent generations.

Sustainable human development is basically a holistic concept that refers to, among other things, the improvement of living conditions for everyone, inclusive development, the coexistence of future generations under conditions of dignity and freedom, the relations between humans and nature, the satisfaction of needs, and social relations themselves, including their forms of government.

Sustainable human development is at the same time an object of knowledge, a lifestyle, an ethical concept, social relations, the community, the economy, and even a political posture confronting the marketplace. If the danger exists that the concept itself has acquired so many meanings that it ends up losing its content, it is also certain that the evolution of its meaning has allowed for the adoption of multiple views in the course of these years.

Why would it be so important for a Lasallian university to look at sustainable human development as an inspiring element for the work of the university? Precisely because of the very mission of the university that it teach, investigate, impact socially, and, in addition, since the present world circumstances impel it to assume a political mission in its contexts, have an ethical dimension as part of the moral conscience of the society in which it finds itself, and do this from a systematic perspective as part of the cultural system of a society (Silva, 2002).

Sustainable human development allows for the alignment of the Lasallian university mission in such a way that its contribution to the educational process of young people and its impact on the surroundings is more significant. In its teaching function, it allows for the undertaking of many processes with one perspective, first of humanizing, but fundamentally one that carries a social proposal, a posture facing the prevailing economic models that seem to be clearly unsustainably expensive for future generations and that allow the dialogue across disciplines that is so needed to understand the complexity of the human phenomenon in all processes. In its investigative function, sustainable human development is a product of knowledge. In the case of the Lasallian university, a clear option of its research projects has to be in the service of the construction of a society that is inclusive, just, sustainable over time, respectful of the environment, and a facilitator of the dignity of the individual. And, by extension, it allows for the articulation of projects and gives focus to the Lasallian options "par excellence": the poor, the young, and the democratization of knowledge.

In the same way, sustainable human development carries with it a political position that the Lasallian university should assume. Education cannot be isolated from its huge political implications and its obligation to transform structures. We cannot continue to educate using the prevailing system, which, under close examination, is not sustainable over time. This system not only relies upon the concentration of wealth, it also supports models of environmental devastation, the destruction of the social fabric where solidarity isn't possible, the facilitation of consumerism, extreme egotism, and the destruction of the planet along with its natural processes. Certainly, the values of the Gospel and its consequent ethics can be considered and proposed in a way that is humanizing, sustainable, and in accordance with Creation and the dignity of humankind.

The Promotion of Justice, Peace, and the Right to Life

The historic composition of what is called the "global village" has deep roots in modernism, even if it doesn't share a homogenous understanding around the world. The implications of a global village are legion. To understand it and confront the challenges that it poses economically, politically, culturally, and educationally comes not only from university thought, but also from the thinking of the Church and Lasallian thinking. One challenge that directly impacts the mission of the Institute is the promotion of the culture of life and peace, which, far from showing improvement, has increasingly deteriorated over the years. While this challenge has implications in many other sectors and agencies of the international community apart from education, resolution of these issues must also involve higher education. Universities are places where those who make local, regional, and global decisions on those topics are ethically formed. This is to say, some functions that involve the university, such as the fight against corruption and in favor of authentic social justice, life, solidarity, and peace, are really functions that directly correspond to the political realm.

The composition of the global village has acquired some strong connotations in the last fifty years as to what is economic, political, and cultural. In the first instance, the tendency to the unification of the economy around basically financial interests within a neoliberal model; next, the tendency of international politics to total interdependence and unipolarity; and, finally, in the area of culture, the revolution of communications, the unimaginable development of virtual reality and the articulation between these scientific, technological, and economic aspects in connection with the designated societies of knowledge.

At this moment all these aspects have repercussions on the Lasallian university and on the theme of fairness, as well as that of national and international solidarity. This concern for educating for justice, life, peace, and solidarity isn't recent. For decades it has been an important and constant theme within the Institute. Such emphasis must be considered in light of what results have been generated and the degree to which different Lasallian Districts have been transformed. In the case of Lasallian university institutions, one can ask, to what degree have they been sensitive to these issues and responsive to the situations they face?

The direction and messages of both the latest General Chapters as well as Br. Álvaro Rodríguez with respect to this theme (Pastoral Letters and Message to the Universities) are very explicit; likewise, the tasks established by PERLA in the RELAL districts. The first encyclical of Pope Benedict XVI (DCE, 2006) points out definite criteria for the interdependence among justice, solidarity, charity, and beneficence. The previous pope proposed to the world the idea of the globalization of solidarity. Perhaps what it left to do today is to review the priorities of our institutions in light of these criteria and review the interaction of Lasallian universities, by regions and on the international level, in light of these directions and criteria.

Dialogue of the University in Favor of the Rights of the Child and Young People

The contemporary world has developed a special sensitivity for the rights of the child, of women, and, to a lesser degree, of young people. This is seen in international legislation and literature—especially in journalism—and in the number of national and international organizations established to defend and promote these rights. However, it is also evident that there is still a wide gap between the theoretical, legal discourse and the historical reality. This situation has posed a great challenge to the Institute that is translated once again into commitment, especially after the 43rd General Chapter, a commitment that has already produced some amazing results (Ruiz, 2006). Lasallian higher education is summoned to participate in this commitment; however, except for those Institutions that already have existing programs of pedagogy and psychology that have had to deal with the theme of childhood, we have no significant accomplishments to point out.

One of the greatest advances in the modern era has been the study of not only the psychological, sociological, and psycho-pedagogical conditions of children and youth, but also of the ethics of the human rights of these sectors. Current theories contrast with the corresponding understandings of these sectors during the seventeenth and eighteenth centuries.

We certainly no longer see children as miniature adults, *tabulae rasae*, or as savages that need to be domesticated, but rather as subjects endowed with rights that, in some cases, even have priority over other rights of society because on them falls the hope of many societies. Notwithstanding, in other societies, children are still considered a social challenge due to their demographic explosion and the lack of strategies to confront such growth. The Institute, in its mission to uphold the human and Christian education of children and young people, and to support the preferential option of the poorest, has placed our institutions of education, and especially the Lasallian universities, in a somewhat difficult position due to the fact that they know they no longer attend primarily to children but rather to young people. This problem is further complicated by financially restricting the access of poor people to this education.

Comparing university to primary education, there is more of a possibility that young people will be attended to by higher education, and increasingly fewer opportunities for children. However, we can see this matter beyond the possibilities of direct attention, that is to say, through access to Lasallian universities or the pertinent pedagogy for this level—without neglecting the importance of this focus—and pose it from the perspective of being Lasallian universities that are actors of social ethics and politics of the societies where they offer their services.

In this perspective, Lasallian universities can contribute to the discourse with the state as well as with the civil society in relation to the themes of childhood and youth. Such institutions will be valid interlocutors because they back up their proposals with both research and consistent creative imagination, through which they can contribute the motivations that gave rise to the Institute, the experience of more than three centuries of specialized treatment of these sectors of society.

To this end, the creation of a network of "Lasallian Observatories of Childhood and Youth" in strategic places in the world that are home to Lasallian universities takes on geopolitical and strategic importance. Understandings will be established on research, formation, production, compilation, and communication about childhood and youth that will help to support the Lasallian university mission. Social observatories allow for the construction of up-to-date systems of information, monitoring, and evaluation that will make it possible for universities to track the condition of the poorest and youngest children. Such observations will be instruments that facilitate the permanent knowledge of actual conditions where the poorest children and young people are found. This will allow the universities to establish real interventions in order to transform the conditions of the designated priorities of Lasallian charisma (Neira y Martínez, 2005).

The importance of this theme belies its urgency. For that reason, Lasallian universities continue to hold great promise in this field, and they are called upon to develop and increase the programs that attend to these priority sectors of our educational commitment.

By Way of Conclusion

We can affirm, paraphrasing De La Salle, that "Lasallian higher education is of the greatest need." Nevertheless, Lasallian higher education's success will be measured by its social impact in the world today. The Lasallian university has many possibilities: it has qualified human resources, possibilities of exchange with national and international organisms, groups of researchers that can generate projects conducive to the inclusion and the solution of the problems of poverty, capacity to innovate its programs, and influence in the formation of young professionals with not only the technical tools but, above all, the human tools needed for the integral improvement of our societies. Finally, it has the possibilities that few institutions have of living the dream of De La Salle to democratize knowledge and impact the development of nations.

Br. Álvaro Rodríguez, Superior General, has been emphatic in his interventions in universities on the historical role of these institutions. He has made direct appeals to clearly assume concrete options where the historical viability of our universities is in play:

> You can support projects of integral development by making all of your actors more professional, better preparing your educators and evangelizers, evaluating existing programs, generating new research, presenting new alternatives, helping to find new financial resources that permit new initiatives to function in benefit of the poorest and the marginalized, being interlocutors before national and international organisms.

> As Lasallian Universities it is important to ask ourselves if we are active agents of development that is sustainable, environmental, social, economic, political, cultural, and religious. I would like to

invite you to live looking forward, without forgetting your roots, to imagine new ways to respond to the problems of today, by being creative in your initiatives and offerings to those who are left out of the benefits of the globalization that we are living in today—new roads, stimulating initiatives, alternatives capable of giving meaning to their lives. (2005)

The principles of PERLA, even though it originated in Latin America and proposed for our university action, can also be read in other historical contexts. In fact, in the globalized world, there are few topics that can be called "exclusive." These reflections are aimed at helping increase our recognition that education, and in a very specific manner higher education, should have clear objectives in their proposals, daring options in their programs, definite lines in their research, and ethical and political presence in the societies where they develop. Only in this way will it be worthy of the millenary tradition of the university and the tercentennial tradition of the Lasallian option to transform the world through education.

Acknowledgments

I'd like to express my thanks to Fabio Coronado, FSC, and to Luis Enrique Ruiz for their contributions and collaboration. This is a work of collective reflection and construction.

Author Biography

Br. Carlos G. Gómez Restrepo worked as a teacher in various high schools in Colombia, after which he assumed increasingly significant educational and administrative roles including that as president of the Central Technical Institute. He was selected to serve as the executive secretary for the Lasallian Latino-America Region and currently is the vice rector of Universidad de La Salle in Bogotá, Colombia.

Bibliography

Benedicto XVI. Carta Encíclica Deus Caritas Est. Roma. 2006.

Celam. IV Conferencia General del Episcopado Latinoamericano. Santo Domingo, 1992.

Coronado Padilla, Fabio Humberto, FSC. "La Universidad de La Salle: Comunidad educadora de intelectuales católicos." Conferencia pronunciada en el CPL (Curso de Pedagogía y Lasallismo) II Nivel para Docentes. Universidad de La Salle. Bogotá. 7 de Diciembre de 2005.

———. "La Universidad de La Salle: Comprometida con los más pobres del país." Conferencia pronunciada en el CPL (Curso de Pedagogía y Lasallismo) II Nivel para Docentes. Universidad de La Salle. Bogotá. 9 de Diciembre de 2005.

Estatuto Orgánico. Universidad de La Salle. Bogotá. 2005.

Neira Sánchez, Fabio Orlando y Martínez Posada Jorge Eliécer. "Observatorio Lasallista Sobre Niñez y Juventud." Proyecto. Universidad de La Salle. Bogotá. 2005.

Organización de las Naciones Unidad. PNUD. "Informe de Desarrollo Humano." 1994.

PID. (Plan Institucional de Desarrollo 2003–2010). Universidad de La Salle. Bogotá. 2003.

Proyecto Eductivo Regional Lasallista Latinoamericano (PERLA). RELAL (Región Lasallista Latinoamericana). 2002.

Rodríguez Echeverría, Álvaro. Mensaje a la Relal. Asamblea de la Región Lasallista Latinoamericana. Febrero de 2001.

———. Carta a las Instituciones Lasallistas de Educación Superior en América Latina y el Caribe en la fiesta de nuestro Padre y Fundador San Juan Bautista de La Salle. Mayo 15, 2003.

———. "La Educación Universitaria dentro de la Misión" Lasallista. Mensaje a las Universidades. Barcelona. Enero de 2005.

Ruiz, Luis Enrique. "La Educación superior como educación lasallista." CILA (Centro de Investigaciones Lasallistas). Bogotá. Enero de 2006.

Silva, Eduardo. "Sentido y misión de la Universidad Latinoamericana." En Reflexiones sobre Educación Superior. Relal. 2002.

UNIVERSIDAD LA SALLE'S CONTEMPORARY MISSION: TO BE A PLACE OF COEXISTENCE FOR MANKIND

By: Enrique Aguayo

Introduction

Resulting from various phenomena, different social groups are created in contemporary societies. Between them, an abyss grows every day: whites and blacks, poor and wealthy, theists and atheists, educated and ignorant, etc. Such divisions cause social strife that end with the domination of the strongest over the weakest: rich over poor, white over black, educated over ignorant, and so on.

The mission of Universidad La Salle, in imitating Jesus, is to promote human unity.[1] There are no rich or poor, only brothers who work for their mutual good. The white man does not enslave the black man; rather, they live together fraternally; the educated instruct the ignorant, etc., that is to say, that everyone may "be one in Jesus Christ."[2]

Let us study the mission of Universidad La Salle, taking into account two topics: the university in and of itself, and Universidad La Salle: a place of coexistence for mankind (rich and poor, black and white, etc.).

---

[1] Cf. *Jn.* 17: 21; *Rom.* 12: 5.

[2] Cf. *Gal.* 3: 28.

I. The University In and Of Itself

Regarding the university, we will deal with (1) its essential goal, (2) the university and its country, (3) the university professions, (4) the interdisciplinary aspect of the university, and (5) the Catholic university.

1. The University's Essential Goal

The university's essential goal is to benefit the members of society. Be it public or private, confessional or lay, military or civil, the university has the same goal: to offer goods to members of society.

The motive for this is simple: at the conclusion of his/her studies, the university graduate will be inserted into a region of society where he/she will practice the knowledge and skills developed during the course of his/her studies. The benefit received by society results from the application of said knowledge and skills. These benefits are multiple:

- Education that spans from higher education to preschool. Indeed, the university graduate will generate the sort of education children receive in various stages of their life.

- Researchers who permanently renew knowledge.

- Avoiding difficulties that may affect a portion of society, as is the case of medicine in its preventive aspect.

- Solutions to various problems facing a segment of society.

As a whole, the application university graduates give to their formation tends to create the common good: food, shelter, clothing, education, social security (public lighting, police force, firefighters), etc., from which each and every member of society may benefit. From here we go to the appearance of a just society: each one of its members has the necessary goods to live with dignity and each performs her/his job to produce the common good.

2. The University and Its Country

The benefits contributed by the university are those required by the people who make up the country in which it is located. Therefore, the university has to pay close attention to the community in order to discover its needs and generate the knowledge the people are to study. Even more, if we keep in mind its preventive function, the university must detect these needs before they surface, in order to develop, early enough in advance, professions and study areas that, once applied, will create the goods necessary to satisfy them. This is what happens with economic science: it detects the goods that need to be produced before the members of society request them. This also happens with jurisprudence: it formulates laws to regulate possible conducts assumed by the citizens.

3. University Professions

Having at its heart both the people's needs and the goods to satisfy them, the university renews its study plans, generates new professions to study, proposes subjects for research, etc. This is how the leader of a country, in many cases, graduates as a university alumnus; the politicians (members of congress, senators, members of parliament) in charge of finances, of fund collection to defray the costs of public spending (economists, accountants), of caring for this money (administrators), of making laws to give order to people's social conduct (lawyers), etc.; the people responsible for health care (doctors, nurses, chemists); city builders (architects, engineers) acquired their knowledge at the university.

4. The Interdisciplinary Aspect of the University

Given that the needs to be satisfied by the members of society are many and varied—which makes them complex—interdisciplinary cooperation is required. In other words, a dialogue between university students devoted to diverse areas of knowledge must be achieved. This is called dialogue between sciences. This is what happens between the doctor and the chemist, the architect and the civil engineer, the philosopher and the pedagogue, and so on.

But that dialogue should not be restricted to professions. It must be extended to all persons and not only professionals. It is here that the possibility for dialogue between people of diverse cultures in the same country or in different countries arises, or dialogue between individuals of different social classes.

5. Catholic University

Everything that has been said previously becomes a reality here. In addition, the Catholic university includes the dialogue between the sciences and theology, in what is known as the faith-culture dialogue.

For the Catholic Church, the Catholic university is the space where there is dialogue with both Catholic and non-Catholic people, in order to familiarize them with the message of salvation. Consequently, the Catholic university adds to the university's objectives that of ensuring members of society are directed toward and reach God, which is to say, that they are saved.

The dialogue between the sciences, and between them and theology, only takes place if the Catholic university creates an environment where the evangelical values of love and freedom prevail. This is necessary in order to allow university professors, researchers, and students to have the knowledge of their different areas of study plus the knowledge of the world, of life and of man, illuminated by faith. The integration of knowledge is fundamental, since it generates a coherent vision of reality and its parts.

Referring to the common good, the integrated knowledge of the different university graduates (philosophers, engineers, psychologists, physicists) manufactures goods to satisfy each and every one of the people's needs. Lack of integration leaves the community empty of goods. This happens, sometimes, with government leaders: they worry about imposing a certain economic order, and they forget about education or social security; they focus their attention on establishing a legal order, and they forget about the economy, etc. In other words, in lacking integrated knowledge, they govern from a single stance: economic, or legal.

II. Universidad La Salle

To discover Universidad La Salle's contemporary mission we shall analyze seven topics: (1) its identity, (2) its origin, (3) Christian education, (4) Saint John Baptist de La Salle's educational model, (5) the evangelical values applied in Lasallian pedagogy, (6) Universidad La Salle: a place of coexistence for mankind, and (7) the evangelical values Universidad La Salle must promote.

1. Identity of Universidad La Salle

When we speak of identity, we refer to the particular elements of Universidad La Salle that set it apart from other universities, public or private, confessional or lay. The identity is a group of characteristics that define Universidad La Salle. In other words, a Universidad La Salle graduate is known—in his/her treatment of others, in his/her way of practicing his/her profession, in his/her way of speaking, etc.—through the distinguishing traits.

2. Origins of Universidad La Salle

The inspiration for Universidad La Salle is Saint John Baptist de La Salle, whose charisma, spirituality, and pedagogical models permeate the Lasallian system. As a priest, De La Salle founded schools that have roots in Christ, the Gospel, and the Church.[3] These roots come with the practice of Christian values.

---

[3] Cf. Tazzer de Schrijver, Lucio, FSC, *La identidad propia de nuestras instituciones de educación superior*, col. Reflexiones Universitarias, No. 19, Ed. Universidad la Salle, México, D. F., s/f, p. 8.

3. Christian Education

The Lasallian educational project is based on a Christian worldview[4] that educates without losing sight of Jesus and his Gospel. In other words, the Lasallian professor educates with evangelical criteria. For example, the professor demonstrates love for the student as a person needing knowledge and is attentive to his/her needs. In Christ's style, the Lasallian professor is attentive to the student's educational needs in order to transmit knowledge, help develop skills, etc.[5]

That attention is extended to provide the student with the necessary goods to satisfy his/her needs and those of the people around the Lasallian teacher. From here, the student becomes a researcher: he analyzes, from his formation, the reality in which he is immersed, and he proposes ways to solve difficulties by going directly to the root of the problem. This is not about giving some coins to the needy, but the creation of jobs (the latter will be done by those with economic resources). Here is Universidad La Salle, creating a place of coexistence between the poor and the rich.

4. Educational model of Saint John Baptist de La Salle

Attentive to the people's needs, De La Salle realized a significant portion of the people did not have access to education because of a lack of economic resources. He devoted his energies to educating them. Does it follow that the rich were excluded from Lasallian education? No, because they have something in common with the poor: ignorance. So the rich are also poor inasmuch as they lack education. Because of this, Universidad La Salle is a space where rich and poor coexist and both benefit from education and mutual help. Accordingly, everyone who wishes to learn and coexist with people of different cultures, social groups, etc., is welcome at Universidad La Salle.

---

[4] Idem.

[5] That attention to the needs of others is seen, clearly, in *Lc.* 7:11-17, where Jesus resurrects the son of Naim's widow: the passage shows Christ to be attentive to the widow's needs, which is why he helps her. The text does not say the widow asked for his assistance; perhaps she did not even know Jesus. He, upon seeing her, takes pity on her and resurrects her young son.

5. Evangelical Values Applied in Lasallian Pedagogy

Let us highlight two evangelical values: justice and fraternity.

Justice. Currently, Universidad La Salle provides education both to the rich and to the poor in order to restore "equality between mankind[6]." As such, Lasallian education is inclusive: it brings together the rich and the poor, Christians and non-Christians. Therefore, it provides space for the coexistence of mankind.

Fraternity. Today, Universidad La Salle promotes fraternity, which makes it a crucible where the haves and the have-nots come together as human beings and recognize each other as equals, as brothers, as children of the same Father who has created them and who gives them a salvation that transcends material wealth or poverty.[7]

6. Universidad La Salle: A Place of Coexistence for Mankind

It is important to bring the rich and the poor together in order to avoid a rift in society, or to keep it from growing. Indeed, by only looking after the poor, we forget the rich. By focusing our attention on the wealthy, we forget the poor. Either position creates a gulf between rich and poor, wherein the latter grow to dislike the former, and the rich become indifferent and insensitive to the needs of the poor. The result is that the poor continue being so and the wealthy remain so. All this is unevangelical: love and justice have been excluded from society.

But if Universidad La Salle opens its doors to both the poor and the wealthy, to Christians and non-Christians, to people of different cultures and races, it will be reducing the gap between the different social, cultural, religious, etc., classes of the country where it is located. That itself

---

[6] Aranda Ramírez, Adalberto, FSC., *El servicio educativo de los pobres y la promoción de la justicia en las Instituciones Lasallistas*, col. Reflexiones Universitarias, No. 51, Ed. Universidad La Salle, México, D. F., 2001, p. 14.

[7] Idem.

introduces the unity of God's children. With regard to this, John Paul II says: Our Father wants the unity of mankind, for which he sent his Son, Who, by dying and resurrecting for human beings, gave them his spirit of love. Christ himself prays to his Father and asks that all his disciples and all who believe in Him, *be united* (cf. *Jn.* 17:21).[8] The model of unity between mankind should be the Holy Trinity.[9]

Based on this, the task or mission of Universidad La Salle, in the contemporary world, is to reduce, little by little, the differences that separate rich and poor, Christian and non-Christian, etc., until they are eliminated.

7. Evangelical Values Universidad La Salle Must Promote

Being of Christian inspiration, the education at Universidad La Salle must be based on evangelical values. In other words, the Lasallian university professor must teach his class without losing sight of evangelical values. Among these, the following stand out, in order of importance and transcendence: love, Christian freedom, justice, common good, and solidarity.

A) Evangelical Love

Christ defines love as: "Giving one's life for one's friends."[10] Giving one's life means two things: to die, physically, for the loved one, and to share with the loved one what one has in life.

---

[8] Cf. Juan Pablo II, *Ut unum sint*, Roma, 1994, § 6, § 9 and § 23; *Euntes in mundum*, Roma, 1988 § 10; *A los religiosos y religiosas de América Latina con motivo del V Centenario de la Evangelización del Nuevo Mundo*, Roma, 1992, § 27. Cf. Aguayo, Enrique, *El amor de Dios Trino y Uno en la teología de Juan Pablo II*.

[9] Cf. Juan Pablo II, *Ut unum sint*, § 8. Cf. Aguayo, Enrique, *El amor de Dios Trino y Uno en la teología de Juan Pablo II*.

[10] *Jn.* 15: 13. Cf. *Jn.* 10:11.

To die, physically, for the loved one. It is what Christ did, by dying on the cross to redeem each and every human being,[11] or what Saint Maximilian Kolbe did, by giving up his life in the concentration camp to keep a father from dying and leaving his wife and children helpless.

To share with the loved one what one has in life. The second meaning of "giving one's life" is to share with others what one has in life: joy, time (to devote to them), unselfish help, knowledge, etc.

This is exactly where love becomes inherent to pedagogical activity. The Lasallian teacher will teach his/her knowledge without restrictions or with the necessary limitations (age of the students, their university scholastic level). He/she will help the student to the maximum level possible, understand and assimilate the transmitted knowledge, develop the required skills, and use the knowledge positively in relation to the knowledge of others. He/she will remain open to teaching students even outside the classroom, if possible, and when the student requests it or when the teacher deems it necessary, he/she will transmit his/her knowledge in the form of morally good advice to guide the student in his/her daily life. In a word, the Lasallian university teacher teaches chemistry or physics or mathematics or biology loving the student, regardless of his/her social class, race, culture, religion, etc.

Punishment. Love for your fellow human being entails fraternal correction. In other words: the student must be corrected, when necessary.[12] The word *castigo* ("punishment" in Spanish) is composed of two Latin words: *castum*, "pure," and *agere*, "make." Therefore, *castigar* (to punish) means "to purify someone." What is the purification from? From mistakes in the science

---

[11] The purpose for Jesus' death on the cross can be read in: Aguayo, Enrique, *El sentido de la muerte de Cristo en la cruz, según Juan Pablo II*, Ed. Basilio Núñez, S. A. de C. V. and Nueva Librería Parroquial de Clavería, S. A. de C. V., México, 2003.

[12] The *Holy Scripture* considers the need for punishment: the New Testament mentions it in *Apo.* 3:19; *1 Cor.* 11:32; *Heb.* 12:4-11; the Old Testament speaks about it in *Prov.* 3:11-12. Likewise, St. John Baptist de La Salle talks about punishment. E.g.: *Carta 36*, § 14; *Carta 55*, § 16 and § 17; *Reglas Comunes de los Hermanos*, ch. VII, § 2; ch. VIII, § 1, § 2 and § 3.

the student is learning, bad behavior, etc. The object of the correction is to direct the student toward [truth and] good,[13] to acquire profound knowledge and to distinguish correctly, good from evil. One must experience the former and avoid the latter.

B) Christian Freedom

Christian freedom consists of neither committing sin nor being a servant to it.[14] Consequently, Christian freedom exists in doing good for oneself and for others. Good is done, among other ways, when the person acquires the values he/she needs to live with dignity and helps others to acquire theirs. Such help is given when opportunities are created so that each and every one of the human beings who surround us can exercise their freedom.

The coexistence of mankind within Universidad La Salle must create a life in common among all, where a mutual interest to help one another prevails. With this we pursue the objective that all have "one single heart and soul,"[15] which results in the interest of each member of the university community for the whole of the university community. Helping each other will generate spaces where there are equal opportunities for each university member to exercise his/her freedom and obtain the necessary goods that will allow him/her to live with dignity.

Once graduated, university alumni will create in the society where they practice their profession, spaces similar to the one they live in at Universidad La Salle. Thus, they encourage the reduction of poverty, racial discrimination, corruption, crime, etc.

---

[13] Cf. San Juan Bautista de La Salle *Carta 11*, § 19.

[14] Cf. Juan Pablo II, *Creo en el Espíritu Santo. Catequesis sobre el Credo III*, tr. L'Osservatore Romano en español, col. Libros Palabra, no. 17, Ediciones Palabra, Madrid, España, ⁵1998, p. 375.

[15] Cf. *Act.* 4:32.

C) Justice

Justice only occurs if the involved parties are, in some way, united. For this reason, Universidad La Salle must be the place where humans co-exist. Of much that has been said about justice, let us review some theses that make the Lasallian teacher and student just.

Definition of justice. John Paul II defines justice as distributing goods "equally, giving each part its share, nothing more and nothing less."[16] Let us explain.

The good to be distributed is of two kinds: temporal, of a material nature, and, in a way of speaking, spiritual. The first comprises a salary, the private property of the home one lives in, etc. The spiritual involves moral goods, such as the acquisition of culture, fame, respect, etc.[17]

The distribution of goods can occur between two humans or between different members of society, generating commutative and distributive justice. Goods must be distributed equally, that is to say, each person should be given his/her due. Justice deals with goods, with things, not with people. When they receive the goods belonging to them, they become equal; they both have their own, nothing more and nothing less.

Applying this to Lasallian university pedagogy, justice is present in a close teacher-student relationship: the teacher begins his/her class precisely at the time scheduled,[18] the student shows up punctually for class[19]; the teacher sets a task or exercise for the student, who must do it, and the

---

[16] Wojtyla, Karol, *Mi visión del hombre. Hacia una nueva ética*, tr. Pilar Ferrer, col. Biblioteca Palabra, No. 2, Ediciones Palabra, Madrid, España, ²1997, pp. 98-99; Juan Pablo II, *Sollicitudo rei socialis*, Roma, 1987, § 26; *Centesimus annus*, Roma, 1991, § 10. Cf. Aguayo, Enrique, "Aproximación al concepto de justicia de Juan Pablo II", en *Vera Humanitas*, no. 39, Ed. Universidad La Salle, México, D. F., 2005, p. 55.

[17] Cf. *Udienza Generale*, Mercoledi 8 novembre 1978, § 4, at http://www.vatican.va/holy_father/john_paul_ii/audiences/alpha/data/aud19781108it.html

[18] San Juan Bautista de La Salle, *Carta 57*, § 11.

[19] Ibid. *Carta*, § 34, 26.

teacher then corrects it.[20] In class, the teacher is just if he focuses on the topic to be taught[21] and avoids speaking of matters foreign to the subject at hand.

Among students, justice appears when they help each other: the one who knows helps the one who does not, the one with the most capacity must help the one with the least capacity. This activity can be initiated by the teacher[22] or by the student himself/herself.

Here we see how the gap that separates the poor from the wealthy, the white from the black, etc., is closed: in the classroom they help each other, and their actions are therefore just. After graduation, when they practice their profession, they will still help each other, which will make the differences between social classes disappear and will gradually generate fraternal and fair coexistence.

Evangelical justice. Because Lasallian pedagogy is of Christian inspiration, we cannot forget evangelical justice. According to John Paul II, such justice is the "acquiesence [of man] with God's will, in the obedience to his laws and in the personal friendship with Him." The divine laws are stated by the Decalogue and the deeds of mercy: they are summarized in the love for Him and others as for oneself. Consequently, he who loves fulfills God's will[23] and practices evangelical justice. According to this, justice is completed by love. Even more, to be just, we must love first.

Applying the aforementioned to Lasallian university pedagogy, evangelical justice happens in the classroom when the teacher, who loves his/her students, gives them what belongs to them: profound knowledge, updates about the topic to be taught, a good example with his/her behavior, respectful treatment of the student and other members of the community, good appearance in his/her dress, correctness in his/her address, etc.

---

[20] Ibid. *Guía*, 16 and 19.

[21] Ibid. *Guía*, 26.

[22] Ibid. *Guía*, 62.

[23] Cf. Juan Pablo II, *Creo en el Espíritu Santo...*, p. 403. Aguayo, Enrique, "Aproximación...", p. 62.

One way of experiencing evangelical justice is by forgiving insults and offences,[24] correcting the offender,[25] consoling the sad, the depressed,[26] and tolerating each other.[27] Only by living alongside the poor is it possible to realize their needs, their anguish, their depression, and the sadness they suffer because they cannot satisfy their basic needs. Because of this, Universidad La Salle must be a place where the rich and the poor can coexist, so the former can become aware of and sensitized to the poor, so they can help them. For example, when they practice their profession, they will do so in such a way that they tend to eliminate poverty, by offering appropriately paid jobs, good education, better housing conditions, etc.

Social justice. John Paul II defines social justice as "the fair participation of material goods in society and [the] help for the poorest, for all the unfortunate ones." In the fair distribution of material goods, love favors peace and reconciliation among members of society. Social justice equalizes the distribution of goods among groups and equalizes the members of these groups. Said goods form a part of the common good.[28]

At Universidad La Salle, social justice is promoted when students lend each other books, pencils, etc. Depending on what they need at any given moment, the university provides the student and professor study materials (library books, etc.).[29]

Love and justice must complement each other. The aim of justice is that things are to be shared among several people. Love's goal is for people to get close to one another. This is why "love is more perfect than

---

[24] Cf. *Mt.* 18:21-22.

[25] Cf. *Lc.* 17:3.

[26] Cf. *Jn.* 11:20-44; *Lc.* 7:11-15.

[27] Cf. *Ef.* 4:2; *Gal.* 6:2.

[28] Cf. Juan Pablo II, *Creo en la Iglesia. Catequesis sobre el Credo IV*, tr. L'Osservatore Romano en español, col. Libros Palabra, no. 22, Ediciones Palabra, Madrid, España, 1997, p. 191. Aguayo, "Aproximación. . .", p. 58.

[29] Cf. San Juan Bautista de La Salle, *Guía*, 13.

justice"[30]. For example, in a dispute, the judge gives each one his/her due. In other words, he forces the one who has the duty to give the corresponding goods to the one who has the right. If after the dispute is solved, the individuals stop living side by side, it does not matter, as justice has been done. If love is added, after the dispute, both individuals will continue to coexist. Even more, if love prevails, any possibility of harm disappears. That is why Saint Augustine said: "Love and do what you will."

D) The Common Good

The common good is called common because it belongs to many who must share it since all have the right to have it. No one must hoard it for himself/herself.[31] Food, clothing, rest, education, social security, etc., constitute the common good.

The Gospel deals, in some way, with the common good, e.g., in the multiplication of the loaves, which, after being blessed by Christ, are divided among many.[32] Such good is made by each and every member of society under the tutelage of the state, which is in charge of distributing it justly, i.e., to ensure that each member of society has what he/she needs to live with dignity, without deprivation and without the need to beg for it.

But, how do we know which goods others require, how many, and when? This is where Universidad La Salle intervenes. Daily coexistence between students allows them to get to know each other's needs and the type of goods that will satisfy them. While they are still students, rich and poor can help each other to obtain said goods more singularly—one helping another—than socially, but, when they graduate, they will be able, with the practice of their profession, to do something to remedy the needs of larger groups.

---

[30] Cf. Wojtyla, Karol, *Amor y responsabilidad*, tr. Juan Antonio Segarra, S. J., col. Psicología – Medicina – Pastoral, No. 70, Ed. Razón y Fe, S. A., Madrid, España, 1969, p. 98.

[31] Cf. Juan Pablo II, *Carta a las familias*, Roma, 1994, § 11 y § 12.

[32] Cf. *Mt.* 14:13-21; *Mc.* 6:30-44; *Lc.* 9:10-17; *Jn.* 6:1-15. Cf. San Juan Bautista de La Salle, *Guía*, 4.

E) Solidarity

The word *solidarity* comes from solid (*solum*, *-i*), which meaning is "ground, earth," in the sense of "soundness." Solid is what is sound. The etymology shows what is intended when applying the concept to human relations: they must be so close that they cannot be altered. Let us illustrate with a solid body. It is so in the measure that its atoms are linked together in such a way that it proves to be impenetrable: water, air, and other substances cannot go through a steel rail. Something similar must happen between individuals: they must be intimately linked to perform their tasks efficiently, help one another, etc.

The classroom at Universidad La Salle is a good place to promote solidarity and make the students become aware of the importance of carrying out activities with others, permanently.

Solidarity is the "*interdependence*, perceived as a *determining system* in relationships in today's world, in its economic, political, and religious aspects, and assumed as a moral category."[33] Solidarity is a moral category because it benefits others: it directs their behavior toward the common good, earthly and eternal, [e.g.], their final salvation.

From what has just been said, it follows that solidarity "is reached by starting, so to speak, from more restricted human circles, where people show solidarity with each other."[34] This can be seen from the classroom, where joint activities take place (paying attention to the teacher, doing homework and/or exercises), to the help that, through the exercise of a profession, may be given to larger portions of society, such as creating jobs, training people for work, and evangelizing.

The foundation of solidarity is "the mystery of God one and Threefold."[35] Indeed, the core of solidarity is interdependence, i.e., the link between each

---

[33] Cf. *Sollicitudo rei sociales*, § 38.

[34] Cf. Wojtyla, Karol, *La renovación en sus fuentes. Sobre la aplicación del Concilio Vaticano II*, tr. José Luis Legaza, col. BAC NORMAL, No. 430, Madrid, España, 1982, p. 231.

[35] Cf. *Ecclesia in America*, Roma, 1999, § 52.

other. In the Holy Trinity there is an extremely close philetic relationship: the Father loves the Son, who returns this love, from which the Holy Spirit proceeds. So, as the three persons of the Trinity relate to each other, in a similar way, *mutatis mutandis*, must mankind be linked. Love must prevail among them. Thanks to love, they benefit each other, especially the neediest, both in the material and the spiritual, because they are provided with the necessary goods to live with dignity: well-paid jobs, a good and integral education, inexpensive basic products, etc.

Likewise, solidarity rises from the "Son of God, incarnate and dead for all."[36] Indeed, Christ came to the world to free each individual from sin, thereby attracting, to Him, all mankind, thus creating unity. This brings about solidarity or mutual help, since being one, they are close to one another, which allows them to help each other.

Conclusion

Within Universidad La Salle there is a shared mission: to foster the coexistence of humanity, regardless of race, religion, social class. In the words of Br. Juan Pablo Martín, "We [believers] do not exclusively improve the world. We have the responsibility to cooperate with others."[37] As Lasallian university members, we strive to help in the style of Saint John Baptist de La Salle: being inspired by Jesus, his Gospel, and his Church, we experience values such as love, justice, common good, and solidarity, without excluding anyone.

Author Biography

Enrique Aguayo is a member of the philosophy faculty for Universidad La Salle in Mexico City. Professor Aguayo has written considerably on a variety of Catholic themes, notably the texts of Pope John Paul II.

---

[36] Idem.

[37] Cf. Martín Dueñas, Juan Pablo, FSC., *Un proyecto educativo en la justicia y la solidaridad. Primera parte*, col. Reflexiones universitarias, No. 57, Ed. Universidad La Salle, México, D. F., p. 53.

LASALLIAN SCHOLARSHIP AND HIGHER EDUCATION

By: Br. Gerard Rummery

If the Lasallian heritage since its very beginnings has been characterised by its ability "to respond to local needs," as in such instances as the Sunday academies in Paris after 1698, the teaching of elementary navigation to the children of fishermen in Calais after 1703, or the beginnings of double entry bookkeeping to the children of Rouen merchants at Saint-Yon after 1709, the same principle has usually been operative in the foundation and development of various forms of Lasallian higher education in the nineteenth and twentieth centuries.

The founding and directing of teacher-training institutions was a natural corollary to what John Baptist de La Salle did three times in his lifetime to provide teachers for the countryside. The growth and development of some of these very different institutions into particular areas of expertise—colleges and universities in the USA, the Philippines, and Colombia; the polytechnical schools in Lyons and Saint-Etienne and the agricultural Institute at Beauvais in France; the seven Saint-Luc schools of art, architecture, painting, graphic design, and photography in Belgium; the Institute of the Sea in Venezuela; the Saint Pius X Institute of Catechetics at Salamanca and Madrid; and so many others—became different responses to answer the particular needs of place and time before becoming "established" in terms of their individual excellence.

There was no immediate and obvious avenue for the transfer of what might be called traditional and external "Lasallian characteristics" in these tertiary educational institutions where there were sometimes only a few Brothers engaged in face-to-face teaching. Thus, if we consider what would have happened as standard practice in the original elementary schools of the eighteenth and nineteenth centuries, it would certainly be unusual in most tertiary institutions today to recall the presence of God before the beginning of each class, to pray morning or evening prayers, or to offer the traditional "reflection." Taking into account the age of the students, the organisation and nature of tertiary education, and the many different cultures in which Lasallian tertiary institutions are now located, such good-in-themselves practices are no longer appropriate. The perennial question then becomes: How do these tertiary institutions remain recognizably Lasallian?

In attempting to answer this question, I wish to propose that we should be looking for *the values* behind some of the traditional Lasallian practices developed originally for the French primary schools of the late seventeenth and early eighteenth centuries, rather than any attempt to replicate the practices themselves, perhaps with some idea that an underlying uniformity can be maintained. We need, rather, to be creative in developing ways of passing on the values of these traditional practices through various pastoral and pedagogical procedures in today's Lasallian tertiary institutions. The diversity of sociocultural situations in which these institutions function is its own warning against any kind of uniformity, imported or imposed from outside the culture. All of this, I suggest, requires a basic sequence of steps that Lasallians working in tertiary institutions are particularly qualified to follow:

- Learning to know, appreciate, and revisit the founding story so that the extrapolation of Lasallian values is made possible from a deep understanding of the Lasallian heritage.

- Becoming familiar with, and making use of, the extensive resources that have been developed through the critical Lasallian studies carried out since the late 1950s to the present day.

- Developing creativity in rereading the founding story and becoming better informed from the critical studies now available in order to respond to the particular needs of the students in the wide variety of Lasallian tertiary institutions today.

And here those working in Lasallian tertiary institutions have a treasure trove insufficiently known, just waiting to be exploited! Allow me to offer some important keys to this treasure house.

Knowing, Appreciating, and Revisiting the Founding Story

As part of the Institute's continuing research on John Baptist de La Salle and his writings, the General Chapter of 1956 authorised a massive project that aimed to produce critical editions of all the Founder's writings through what were to be called *cahiers lasalliens*, or Lasallian workbooks, some forty-five of them. The direction of this work was entrusted to Br. Maurice-Auguste Hermans, a Belgian Brother and canon lawyer whose doctoral study centered on the Bull of Approbation granted by Pope Benedict XIII for the approval of the existence of the Institute of the Brothers of the Christian Schools. Of course, all this basic research had to be done and published in French. The presence in Rome between 1958 and 1972 of a large number of Brothers from around the world studying theology in the Lateran University provided many of them with an important Lasallian research topic to develop to licentiate [master's] or doctoral level.

Among the early *cahiers lasalliens* were the critical editions of the first biographies of De La Salle, all of which of course were written in French. All of these biographies are now available in modern translations in English and Spanish. The biographies in chronological order are:

- A manuscript written in 1721 two years after De La Salle's death by a Brother Bernard, who had access to written testimonials and firsthand accounts from the Brothers.

- A biography written in 1723 by Dom Elie Maillefer, De La Salle's nephew, mainly to offer something more worthy from the De La Salle family viewpoint than this first attempt by Brother Bernard; this version came directly or indirectly into the possession of the Brothers and was obviously known to Jean-Baptiste Blain, De La Salle's main biographer.

- A three-volume life written by Jean-Baptist Blain in 1733 at the request of Brother Timothy, Superior General. Like De La Salle, Blain trained at Saint-Sulpice, and had known De La Salle in the last four or five years of his life as chaplain at Saint-Yon, where De La Salle died in 1719.

- A second version written around 1740 by Dom Maillefer when he realised that his earlier version had been used by Blain without acknowledgment.

It is evident that all these biographies made use of the same sources as many of the texts cited by the three biographers are exactly the same. Unfortunately, the sacking of the Institute's main house at Melun in 1792 during the French Revolution was probably the occasion when some of the original materials were lost.

As the project gathered momentum through the 1960s and into the 1970s, it became clear that an important tool that needed to be developed was De La Salle's own vocabulary, particularly in deciding whether certain writings attributed to him were in fact his own, because of plagiarised editions of some writings even in his lifetime. But these were pre-computer days! Once the major critical editions had been published, a group of retired French and French-speaking Belgian Brothers were assigned to read particular works and to produce the key words in alphabetical order, citing the particular phrase and indicating its provenance. In a project that lasted around fifteen years, De La Salle's "vocabulary" was eventually established in six volumes. With this most valuable tool now available, it became possible to launch some secondary studies that had assumed more importance in the light of the critical editions now concluded. This explains why the original forty-five volumes have now become some sixty-plus, with a number of others yet in progress.

In the 1930s, Brother Superior General Adrien commissioned M. Georges Rigault, a fellow of the Historical Academy of France, to write the complete history of the Institute of the Brothers of the Christian Schools from its origins. M. Rigault concluded his work in ten volumes in 1952, although the final volume that treated of the secularisation laws of 1905 in France was not published until 1991 because it appeared to reflect badly on the conduct of some of the Superiors who were still alive or only recently dead! This resource is available only to those who can read the original French.

In 1996, at the request of the then Superior General Br. John Johnston and his Council to provide a series of four booklets to provide a general historical overview for young Brothers in formation in different parts of the Lasallian world, Brother Henri Bédel published his first volume of *An Introduction to the History of the Brothers of the Christian Schools*, a series now nearing completion. These texts, published in French, English, and Spanish, stand in their own right as research work of high quality because the author, besides offering a sequential narrative, has skilfully treated the main questions faced by the Institute at various moments in its three-hundred-plus years of growth and development.

Current general publications from the centre of the Institute in French, English, and Spanish include the *Bulletin of the Institute of the Brothers of the Christian Schools*, *Intercom*, and various booklets on aspects of the Lasallian mission known as MEL Bulletins [MEL = *mission educative lasallienne*]. These publications can now be accessed from the Institute's Web site at *lasalle.org*, along with Circular Letters from the Superior General and Council and news items from around the Lasallian world.

Most districts of the Institute have published detailed histories of their foundation and development.

The Fruits of This Research

The impetus of the original research projects initiated by the General Chapter of 1956 has continued. One extraordinary contributor to this research has been Br. Léon Aroz, Catalan by birth, a renowned French scholar, whose work has twice been officially honoured by the French government. It was his painstaking research that located the original journals and account books that the young John Baptist de La Salle had to submit each year when he was named executor of his father's will while he was still technically a minor. Through an astonishing series of now some twenty-five *cahiers*, Aroz has enabled us to discover so many details of the life and transactions of the young De La Salle from 1670 to 1678, when he was carrying out his executor's duties. These detailed insights into the young De La Salle at twenty-one years of age taking on responsibilities and making important decisions have helped us discover, in

Michel Sauvage's words, "not so much the saint as the *man* who became a saint!" Aroz has also greatly enriched our knowledge and understanding of the family history of De La Salle's mother and father and of Jean-Baptiste's own siblings.

As the fruit of the critical research initiated during the 1950s, a number of modern biographies based on these sources are now available in different languages. Among the most important sources that have enlarged our knowledge of the social, political, and educational forces at work during the foundation period, there stands the two-volume doctoral thesis of Br. Yves Poutet, *Le XVIIe siècle et les origines lasalliennes* [*The Seventeenth Century and Lasallian Origins*], published in 1970.

The main lines of the detailed work done by Aroz and Poutet can be read in English in a series of excellent books by Br. Luke Salm, who also prepared the English edition of Blain's three volumes. Salm published *Beginnings: De La Salle and his Brothers* [incorporating in detail translations from Aroz, Poutet, and Jean Pungier]; *Encounters: De La Salle at Parmenie*, in 1982; *The Formative Years*, in 1989; and in the same year, the biography entitled *The Work Is Yours: The Life of Saint John Baptist de La Salle*.

Poutet's work was also the basis for Br. Alfred Calcutt's impressive biography of the 1990s, entitled *De La Salle: A City Saint and the Liberation of the Poor through Education*. This is a single volume in English of over five hundred pages that places De La Salle and his first Brothers against the background of Louis XIV and the late seventeenth century.

The critical editions of all of De La Salle's works in French have made it possible between 1980 and 2000 for these same editions to be translated and published in English and Spanish, thus making the fruits of more than thirty years of research available in the three main languages used in the Institute. Many of these works have also been translated into Italian. In addition, the Lasallian Studies Commission in the 1980s launched two more important resources. First there were, at two different stages through the 1980s and 1990s, fifty editions of *Lasalliana*, close to one thousand single articles on particular topics, usually on two sides of an A4 sheet to facilitate duplication of multiple copies. These articles, published in French, Spanish, and English, covered a wide range of Lasallian topics from historical articles [e.g. where did the expression *Live, Jesus, in our hearts* originate?] to accounts of current initiatives from all over the Lasallian world. At an academic level, there have been three volumes of *Lasallian Themes*, with a fourth volume still nearing completion.

Lasallian Themes should be of particular value to all Lasallians working in tertiary institutions as all the articles have been produced in French, Spanish, and English. The themes, written by Lasallian scholars from around the world, were written according to specific criteria and had to pass the scrutiny of an international editorial committee. Here, simply by way of example, are some thirteen key themes of the one hundred so far published that have been found to be particularly important in formation sessions with teachers who wish to deepen their Lasallian understanding and commitment.

- **Child-Scholar-Disciple** shows how De La Salle's original view of the nature of the relationships with children in the first schools changes through the sequence of these words from his earlier to his later writings.

- **Correction** shows the enormous and highly significant difference between the treatment of this topic in the 1706 manuscript copy of the *Conduct of Schools*, which is mainly about degrees of the corporal punishment customary at the time, and the development of the idea of correction, which makes this become the longest chapter and in many ways the most significant chapter of the 1720 printed edition.

- **Conduite or Conduct** establishes the seventeenth-century sense of the word often used by De La Salle, as in his last words, "*J'adore en toutes choses la conduite de Dieu en mon égard*" [I adore all the ways in which God has *led and guided* me].

- **The Spirit of Faith**, given by De La Salle as the spirit of the Institute.

- **Catechism**, showing how De La Salle and the first Brothers developed and transformed the traditional method of Saint Sulpice by basing it on better educational principles.

- **Christian Teacher**, a portrait of such a teacher in Lasallian terms.

- **Goodness-Tenderness**, an insight into the particular countercultural climate of Lasallian schools where the Brothers were to be *"brothers to one another in the community"* and *"older brothers to the children confided to them by God."*

- **Hearts: to touch hearts**, the special relationship required of being a true Lasallian *brother or sister* in relationships with students.

- **The Reflection**, that particular special moment in the first schools where the usually silent teacher spoke from his heart to the hearts of students.

- **Salvation**, De La Salle's concern for the spiritual and temporal care of the children whom he saw as "far from salvation."

- **Vigilance**, the basis of De La Salle's preventative pedagogy that was to influence many other founders, especially Saint Don Bosco.

- **Zeal**, the spirit of faith in action.

- **Minister/Ministry**, De La Salle, basing himself on Saint Paul, anticipated the contemporary use of the term in Pope John Paul's *"Lay People Faithful to Christ"* to describe the work of the Christian educator.

Some Implications for Lasallian Institutes of Higher Education

Under the title *Lasallian Resources: Current Lasallian Studies*, the USA/ Toronto Region commissioned and had published a number of important critical studies, including the following:

- *Saint John Baptist de La Salle and Special Education: A Study of Saint Yon*, by Br. Othmar Worth.

- *So Favored by Grace: Education in the Time of John Baptist de La Salle*, a collection of seven articles all written by Brothers.

- *Spirituality in the Time of John Baptist de La Salle*, including the translation into English of two important articles of André Rayez,

SJ, former editor of the French Dictionary of Spirituality, and further translations from Brs. Yves Poiutet, Maurice-Auguste, and Michel Sauvage, plus an article by Br. Luke Salm on Lasallian charism.

All of these articles were written by Brothers, and the publications were edited by Brothers associated with Lasallian institutes of higher education. In my many years of presenting aspects of the Lasallian heritage in programmes of the International Lasallian Centre and International Sessions of Lasallian Studies in Rome, in the Buttimer and Lasallian Leadership Institutes in the USA/Toronto Region, in the two modified Buttimer programmes run in Great Britain, Ireland, and Malta, and my present work as presenter in the Narooma sessions conducted in District of Australia, New Zealand, and Papua as well as other sessions in the Pacific-Asia Region, I have never ceased to marvel at the impact of the Lasallian story on many different kinds of people. Yet, with the exception of some recent retreats with some faculty members from a particular Lasallian institution, out of all these activities, I can recall only some fifteen to twenty participants from Lasallian institutes of higher education.

The founding story of De La Salle and the first Brothers has transcended the boundaries of language and culture and has its own resonance with many Lasallians who do not share the Catholic faith. I have been deeply moved when Buddhist teachers in a Pacific-Asia Regional meeting in Hong Kong in 1997 told me that they see De La Salle *as a Buddha: a man who was enlightened to see that the value of life was not in wealth, power or status, but in devoting one's life to those less fortunate.* I have had the privilege of knowing two Muslim teachers who, in the spirit of the Koran, have chosen to teach gratuitously in Lasallian schools for many years so that their salaries pass discreetly, without their ever touching the money, to the fund for needy students, most of whom are poor Christians. My life has been enriched on those occasions when I have presented the Lasallian story to young volunteer graduates in the USA and have later seen them in direct service with the poor in various projects or in the foundation and growth of the San Miguel school movement that is so dependent on their generosity.

All these initiatives—service of the poor, gratuity, being *brother and sister*—are present-day ways of implementing Lasallian values that are part of an extremely rich heritage. I have no doubt that there are already many comparable activities in the diverse forms of Lasallian higher education. I am aware of the way in which some Lasallian institutions teaching the popular MBA course [Master of Business Administration] have invoked Lasallian attitudes to the poor as an important component of the course. I am aware that in at least one Lasallian institution, the course is given gratuitously by the professors themselves to a particular group of evening-class students. That is why I applaud the opportunity provided by IALU to share reflections on this topic because if there are already so many foundation Lasallian principles being applied in many different ways, we seem as yet to lack a regular common forum in which to express them. Here, simply by way of suggestion, are some themes for investigation by Lasallians who see themselves associated with and committed to *the Lasallian mission of human and Christian education*:

- There are still many valuable research articles in French that have not yet found a translator into other languages.

- In the USA, the educational writings of Parker Palmer continue to have an important impact on teacher education. Without detracting in any way from their excellence, I have been struck by just how much of what is valuable in this writing can be read in *The Conduct of Schools*, written in 1706 by De La Salle and "the oldest and most experienced teachers." This extremely practical foundation text has its important place in the classics of western education, but is far less known than the much more theoretical Jesuit *Ratio studiorum*, written for a very different clientele.

- *The Twelve Virtues of a Good Master*, written by Brother Agathon in 1785, grew out of his attempts to update the *Conduct*, was translated into six different European languages, and had an extraordinary influence for well over 150 years on the training of teachers in Europe. We are still awaiting an analytical study that would seem to come most naturally from an institute of Lasallian higher education.

- The current interest in the founding concept of Lasallian *association* has already generated a number of important studies from Brothers, but we are still awaiting the important insights from the numerical majority of stakeholders in the present-day Lasallian mission, lay associates.

- All Lasallians would benefit from longitudinal studies of the impact of movements such as the San Miguel schools in the USA, the many programmes being run by Lasallians in many different corners of the world on behalf of street children, the young people in the various Boys Towns.

- Sociological studies on the impact of mixed communities—Lasallian volunteers usually with a small number of Brothers—on the lives of the volunteers and on the lives of the Brothers, and on the principle first enunciated in the Brothers' General Chapter of 1976, "degrees of belonging" to the mission of the Institute.

The list could go on and on. When De La Salle's major writings—educational and spiritual—are now accessible on the Internet through the Web site, there is no lack of opportunity for the critical studies movement, launched through that important General Chapter decision of 1956, to be taken up and extended through the scholarship coming from the many diverse faculties of Lasallian higher education. Copies of most of the important documents published in English, Spanish, and French by the Institute are available by contacting the Institute's Web site in Rome, *www.lasalle.org*. So, what are you waiting for?

Author Biography

Br. Gerard Rummery was director of the International Lasallian Center (CIL) in Rome, after which he was elected to membership on the General Council of the De La Salle Christian Brothers in Rome. As an insightful contributor to Lasallian formation programs around the world, he has served on numerous international religious commissions. Brother Gerard is an adjunct professor at the Australian Catholic University and is currently a team member of Lasallian Education Services for the District of Australia - New Zealand - Papua, New Guinea.